DRAW
FACES

IN 15 MINUTES

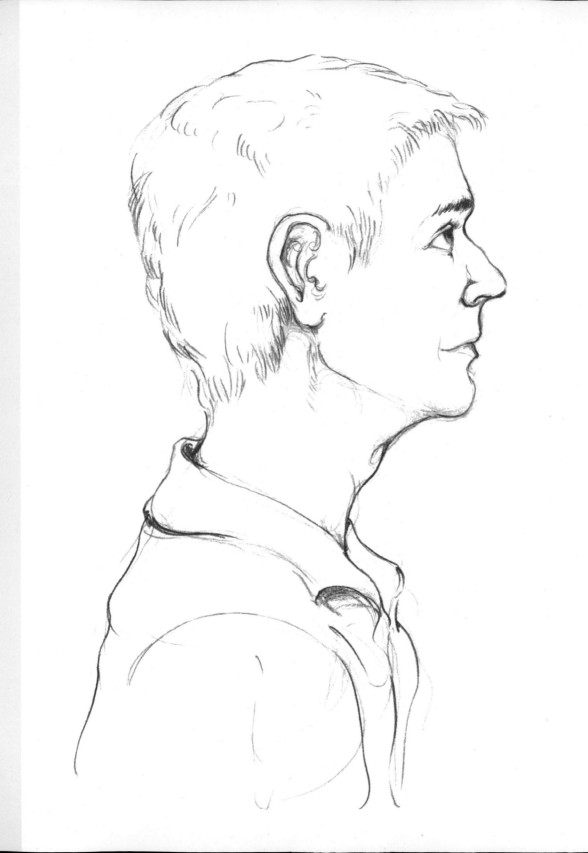

AMAZE YOUR FRIENDS WITH YOUR PORTRAIT SKILLS

DRAW FACES

IN 15 MINUTES

JAKE SPICER

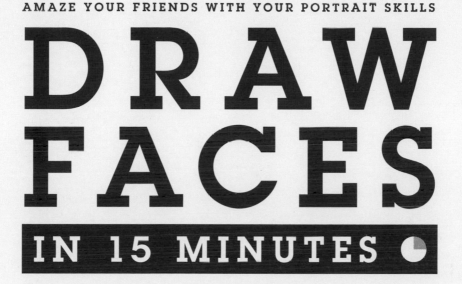

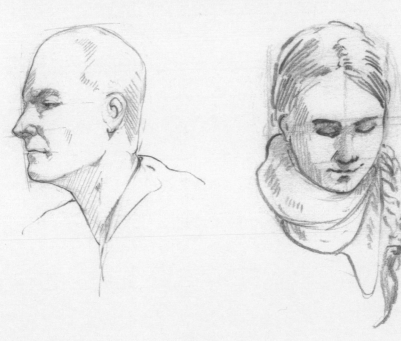

ST. MARTIN'S GRIFFIN
NEW YORK

DRAW FACES IN 15 MINUTES

For information, address St. Martin's Press,
175 Fifth Avenue, New York, N.Y. 10010.
www.stmartins.com

Library of Congress
Cataloging-in-Publication Data
Available Upon Request

ISBN 978-1-250-06399-1

St. Martin's Griffin books may be purchased for educational,
business, or promotional use. For information on bulk
purchases, please contact Macmillan Corporate and
Premium Sales Department at 1-800-221-7945, extension
5442, or write specialmarkets@macmillan.com.

Printed in China.

First U.S. Edition: May 2015

10 9 8 7 6 5 4 3 2 1

This book was conceived,
designed, and produced by
I L E X
210 High Street,
Lewes,
East Sussex,
BN7 2NS
www.ilex-press.com

For Ilex:
Publisher: Alastair Campbell
Executive Publisher: Roly Allen
Editorial Director: Nick Jones
Senior Project Editor: Natalia Price-Cabrera
Commissioning Editor: Zara Larcombe
Senior Specialist Editor: Frank Gallaugher
Assistant Editor: Rachel Silverlight
Art Director: Julie Weir
Designer: Grade Design

Color Origination by
Ivy Press Reprographics

Contents

Introduction

This book is for anyone who has looked at another person and felt the urge to capture their likeness on a piece of paper, or for anyone who has looked at a portrait and envied the draftsman their understanding of the human face. Everyone can learn to draw, and everybody who has started drawing can learn to draw better.

Why Draw Faces?

Nothing fascinates us more than other people; we crave communication and connection. In a world full of secondary images, the process of drawing gives us precious moments to sit down with somebody else and create a response to them with marks on a tactile surface, immediate and raw. We're the cleverest of creatures, and our wish to empathize with our fellow beings through gaze and expressions make us amazingly good at picking up on the subtle detail of human proportions. How better to exercise that ability than to learn to translate what we see into drawings?

The Language of Drawing

An ability to draw is often described as a talent, but it's better to call it a skill. Drawing is a craft that can be learned as easily as any other; it is more like a language than anything else, a way of describing the world visually using a vocabulary of line and tone. Like a spoken language it has a certain grammar or structure that can be learned. This book serves as a guidebook, giving you some simple visual "phrases" to communicate fundamental ideas. But through practice and experience, and regular drawing, you can develop a broader range. In time your marks can become poetic, eloquent, and you will become more fluid in your articulation and your visual description of what you see. Just as learning a verbal language enables you to listen to the language more easily, so learning to draw can make you see the visual world with new clarity.

Beginning

When you first start you'll be clumsy, your pencil stumbling over lines as your tongue might stumble through a foreign phrase. There are some people who find drawing effortless and others who find it difficult—everybody struggles. Some people just enjoy the struggle and work through it, while others give up. The frustration and puzzlement that comes with drawing is a part of the process; it encourages you to seek and be curious. Without a struggle no learning would take place. Through drawing and learning to look, you can open the door to a whole new way of seeing the world. Textures, surfaces, and the play of light become endlessly engaging and able to hold your attention for hours while you try to record them in scribbled marks.

Before launching into this book it's worth reading the next few pages, as they serve as an introduction to drawing and a key to how to use the book. Enjoy.

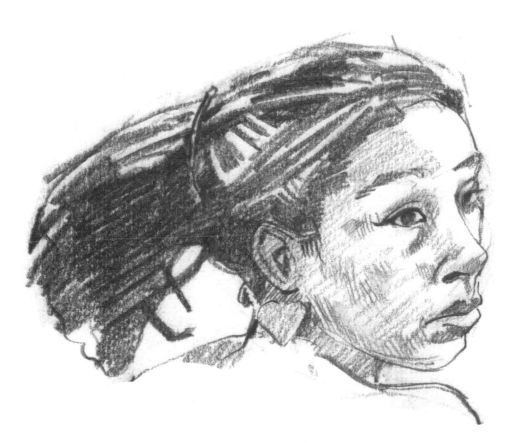

A Face in 15 Minutes

This book aims to give you all the tools you need to draw a decent portrait in about 15 minutes by providing some practical strategies for drawing that can be adapted to suit your needs. The drawing process is a varied and personal journey, and there are many methods for dealing with the problems of the visual world on a piece of paper. There are no hard and fast rules in these pages, and the instruction isn't intended to be dogmatic, although this book does contain well-formulated, practical advice based on teaching hundreds of students.

Why 15 Minutes?

A quarter of an hour is a reasonable time for any sitter to remain still, and a beginner working swiftly will have enough time to lay down the features of the face and structure of the head with room for a few mistakes and corrections. The advantage of a 15-minute portrait over a longer picture is that it's quick enough to capture some life in the sitter's face. The time limit stops your sitter getting fidgety, and you learn to draw lively, engaging portraits. The important thing isn't how long you take to finish your drawing, but how much you learn from doing it.

How to Use the Book

This book is broken down into chapters that explain some of the attitudes and techniques of drawing alongside practical tutorials.

Chapter 1: Introduction—advice on how to set yourself up for the tutorials, with helpful information on basic materials and how to find subjects.

Chapter 2: Learning to Draw—a useful introduction to drawing in general, explaining the techniques used in later chapters using exercises that don't require a model.

Chapter 3: The Basic Portrait Sketch—tutorials that also provide you with the foundation for a more developed portrait; you'll need a model to work from to make the most of this chapter.

Chapter 4: The Developed Portrait Sketch—tutorials on
specific features and sections of the face.
Chapter 5: Taking Your Drawing Further—will help you as
you encounter more visual problems to solve.

The more you practice and the more you draw, the more
in tune your hand will become with your eye; this book
simply gives you a structure for looking, seeing, and
making marks in response to the face. It is a companion
on the road of learning, so don't get lost—use it as a guide
and go find people to draw!

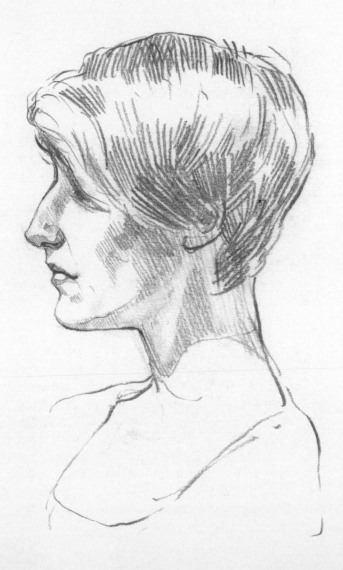

The Model

To start drawing the face you're going to need three things: something to draw on (good quality paper), something to draw with (pencil, sharpener, and eraser), and a face to draw (yourself or a model). Here are some pointers on finding someone to sit for your drawings.

Drawing from Life

Drawing is a way of capturing the essence of a subject on a piece of paper, and the fewer barriers you have to connecting with your model the better. With photography so prevalent, it is very easy to capture somebody's image, but drawing remains as much of a challenge as it ever was. Drawing from a photo is a completely different thing to drawing from life; it disconnects you from the sitter and makes the drawing a monolog of marks, rather than a communication between model and draftsman. When you draw from a photo you are often just copying—from one 2D image to another—but when you're working from life you are really drawing, translating something 3D to something 2D. This books deals with drawing from life, and to make the most of it you'll need to find somebody to sit still and be your model.

So You Need a Model

First of all, don't jump the gun: for your first drawings you need someone who won't mind a few unflattering pictures! Here are some ideas for finding people to draw:

- Try a life drawing class. Even if your aim isn't to study a nude figure, you can concentrate on portraits, and it is an opportunity to see the work of others and share ideas.
- Learn to draw with somebody else. Take it in turns to sit for portraits; you can help one another progress and share tips and revelations. By sitting for a portrait you'll learn to empathize with your models—never a bad thing.
- Find a friend or family member who doesn't mind sitting for a few first portraits. The more you draw one person the better you'll get to know their face, so if you can arrange a regular sitting with them, all the better.

- Practice drawing people on trains or in cafes, or anywhere that they might be likely to stay still and you can sketch them surreptitiously. This is often a good way to keep your sketches loose and playful.
- Use yourself. If you can't find anyone to sit for you, or you want to practice before unleashing your draftsmanship on the world, try a few self-portraits in a mirror.

How to Run a Model Sitting

A portrait session drawing from a model is called a "sitting" and the model a "sitter." Even when it is a very friendly and informal sitting, there are a few things that are always worth bearing in mind, particularly when drawing people who are unused to being drawn.

- Be straight with your model about the level you're at with your portraiture. You will feel more comfortable throwing yourself into drawing in a relaxed way, which will help keep the drawing energetic and interesting.
- Set yourself a time limit for the session; an hour is realistic.
- Sit the model down and chat to them for a few minutes without drawing. Explain what you'll be doing in the drawing and that you need them to remain still, but that they can relax and find a position that is comfortable.
- Once you're ready to start, give your model somewhere to look; this will help them keep their head still. You could even ask them to read a book or watch TV—some kind of background distraction (music or the radio) can really help to relax the model and yourself.
- Try a few short drawings with time limits, and try some different angles of the head to get a composition you're happy with. Use this time to warm up and to learn your model's features.
- After several studies have a break; let the model stretch and then relax back into the pose. Try for a longer portrait, but be strict with your timekeeping.
- You'll often find that in the first studies the model will be holding a forced expression. As you move into the longer pose chat to them, help them relax, and pick up on how their face moves as they talk and smile. If you can bring something of this into your drawings you'll achieve a much more engaging drawing (See Likeness, p. 98).

11

Your Materials

A bad workman might blame his tools, but a good draftsman can be brought down by low-quality pencils and the wrong paper. A "good drawing" made with poor materials on poor paper just isn't a good drawing.

Start simple: pencil and charcoal are staples of drawing because they are versatile and adaptable. Over time you'll find the best materials for you; constantly experiment before you settle on one thing, and once you find something you like, be fussy and make sure you're always equipped with materials that will show your drawings off to the best of their potential. Don't underestimate the importance of the right surface to draw on—different papers will suit different media.

The drawings in this book were all done in graphite pencil on white paper. The techniques described can broadly be applied to most other drawing materials, but you'll find you need to adapt the approaches for different media. A 2B or 3B graphite pencil, a plastic eraser cut in half to give a sharp edge, a sharpener, and 120–160gsm off-white or ivory paper will get the best results from these tutorials.

Here are a few of the common materials you might draw with and a little information about their qualities. Different qualities will suit different styles of working.

Paper

The importance of finding the right paper should not be overlooked. There are thousands of different types to work on and all will suit different media, approaches, or preferences. Look out for the following qualities.

TYPE OF PAPER

Heavy, good-quality drawing paper is ideal to use for drawing; construction paper is cheaper and grainier but often fine. Plain newsprint or lining paper (wall paper) can be used for economy but will age badly. Watercolor paper is absorbent and often textured, and is best used for wet media.

PAPER COLOR

Bleached white is most common, but off-white (ivory or buff) is often preferable as it is more sympathetic to drawn marks and can be highlighted with a white medium. Colored papers can be used, but think about how the tone of your medium will work with the tone of the paper. Printer paper is often a cold, bluish white and should be avoided.

WEIGHT

The weight of paper is important for the feel of the mark on the page, although it doesn't always relate to quality (Japanese papers are very lightweight but can be very expensive). Weight is measured in grams per square meter or gsm, with 120–200 gsm being good weights for drawing paper.

Graphite Pencil

Graphite (lead) pencils have different grades, measured on a scale of 9H–9B with HB in the middle. H pencils are hard, giving pale, faint lines with 9H being the most extreme; Bs are soft, giving dark, grainy, bold lines with 9B being the softest and darkest. Graphite is smooth, gray, and gives a shiny surface. It is very adaptable, can be erased cleanly, and gives a controlled line.

9H 8H 7H 6H 5H 4H 3H 2H H HB B 2B 3B 4B 5B 6B 7B 8B 9B

Harder, lighter ⟵   ⟶ Softer, darker

Pencils should be kept sharp for consistent drawing, but if you want a blunt pencil so that you can achieve a wider, softer line, use sandpaper to wear one edge down.

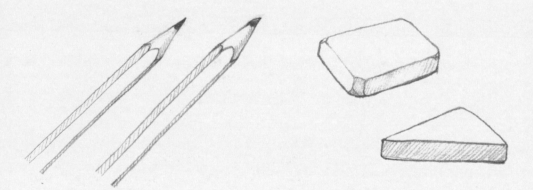

Avoid smudging pencil with your finger; graphite powder is better used for giving soft tone as you can control how it goes on the page. It can be spread with a finger, paintbrush, or shaper.

Erasers

Kneaded erasers come in different grades: hard, medium, and soft. They are malleable, get dark with use, and are best used for erasing charcoal.

Plastic erasers have various qualities with cheap not always meaning bad; test a few to see how cleanly they erase. Cut your eraser to a point so that you can use it as a drawing tool.

Charcoal

Charcoal is black and can be easily smudged. Willow charcoal comes in many different sizes of irregular sticks. It snaps easily and can be used on its side, point down, or crushed up into powder. This medium wants to smudge, and can be rubbed back with the hand and drawn into with an eraser to create light. Because of the difference in surface quality, charcoal doesn't often mix well with graphite and gives a more expressive line.

Compressed charcoal is a dense black medium: it comes in uniform sticks, is harder to smudge, and doesn't erase easily. Conte crayon is a good alternative with similar qualities.

Charcoal pencils are made from compressed charcoal in a pencil casing. They come in different grades either on an HB scale or as light, medium, or dark. They give greater control over lines than other charcoals.

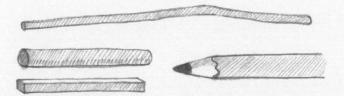

Pen

Most ink pens can't be erased but give clean lines, encouraging bold decisions in drawings. They are good for linear drawings, and water-soluble ink can be wetted with a brush and moved around on the paper for painting in tone.

Ballpoint pens are cheap, versatile, and give a good variety of line. Fountain pens can make ink blots easily and are not always ideal, unless designed for drawing. Finepoint pens give a constant quality of line with better quality inks than ballpoints. Brush pens give a varied weight of line and are tricky to handle but expressive.

LEARNING TO DRAW

Attitudes and Techniques

Attitude

Drawing is mark-making in response to something observed. The attitude you take to a drawing is as important to the outcome as the techniques you use. Every drawing you make should have an intention; a drawing should be created to communicate something about the subject that interests you and that you want to communicate to a viewer. If you can work out what interests you about the model, you can work out how to be selective in making your drawing. Devote your drawing time to the aspects of the sitter that you want to bring out in the sketch; if it is the tilt of the head that particularly engages you, don't spend half your drawing rendering the eye in detail. When you make marks on the page, don't scribble unwittingly, but make each mark the result of a clear, considered thought. The real skill is learning to make considered marks intuitively.

Techniques

"Techniques" in drawing, such as those in this book, are really just frameworks on which to hang your observations of the world. They give you a starting point and a process to work through. They should be a gateway into helping you look at the world properly, not a substitute for looking properly. You should always be aware that you are making a new drawing of someone or something unique, and so shouldn't approach that drawing formulaically.

Style

Style is an elusive thing. Given the same medium and subject, we will all draw something different with our own marks and emphasis, yet it can be hard to pin down what makes each of our drawings unique. Look at the drawings of artists you respect and of other people you know who draw. Learn lessons from their work—how they have solved particular problems, what kind of marks they have made, what they are trying to say about their subject—and use their drawings as a key to understanding how to improve your own. Most of all, don't worry about your style—it will develop in time, and you'll often only recognize it retrospectively when looking over past drawings.

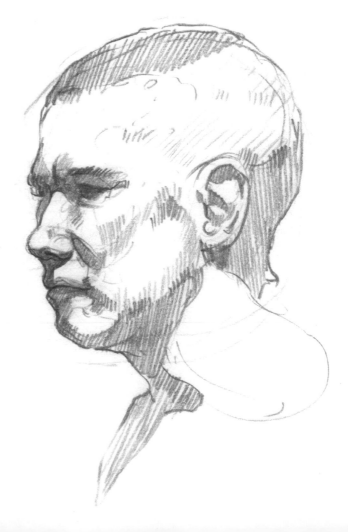

Looking

Learn to Stare

First look, then draw; too often the beginner rushes to make marks before properly seeing the subject. Before looking, make sure you're comfortable and set up to make looking as easy as possible. When you draw, your eyes should be forever flitting from model to paper, paper to model, keeping the dialog between subject and drawing fresh and immediate without the interruption of an internal critical monolog. It is this internal critic telling you your marks are wrong that can restrict drawing much more than a lack of ability. Do everything you can to remain present in the moment of drawing and to maximize the connection between eye and hand without intellect getting in the way.

Develop an Internal Tutor

When you begin drawing, often you'll find you're accompanied by an internal critic, pointing out your mistakes and making you question your drawing. This can be more restricting than a lack of ability. You need time to look and draw without internal criticism. Instead, try to develop an internal tutor, allowing you to stand back and look objectively at your drawing, picking out its best qualities and what can be improved upon.

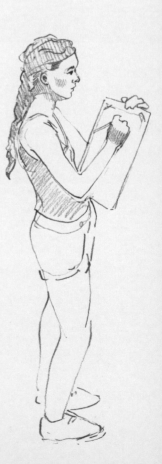

Make It Easy for Yourself

Here are a few different setups to help you draw comfortably. You should aim to keep your paper as close to the plane of your face as possible to avoid distortion as you're drawing. It also helps to minimize the distance your eyes needs to travel between model and paper; if you can see both just by moving your eyes without needing to move your head, then that is ideal.

GUERILLA SKETCHER

If you're out and about sketching, make sure your paper is propped up so that your view of the paper isn't distorted. Use a drawing board to rest your paper on.

SIT-DOWN PORTRAIT

Use the back of a second chair as a support for your drawing board.

AT THE EASEL

Keep the easel upright at forty-five degrees to your body, so you can see model and board at the same time. Avoid playing peek-a-boo with the model.

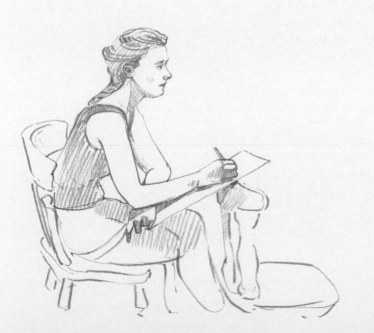

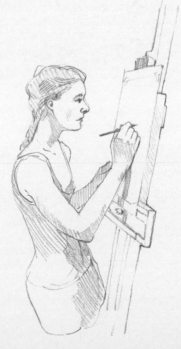

Mark-making

Once your eyes are open to the world around you, you'll need a visual language to describe what you've seen. The marks you make are your way of communicating with the viewer, and to make your drawings coherent you'll need to keep them concise. If you can describe something in one line, don't go back over it three times; if you can describe a face in 100 lines, don't put down 300. The more selective you are with your mark-making, the more easily your viewer will be able to interpret your marks.

Making Marks

When you draw, you tend to make strokes from different parts of your arm. If you can become more aware of how you make your marks, you'll improve the marks themselves. Although your pencil will be moving around the paper all of the time, if you're right-handed, try drawing from the top left of the paper to avoid smudging your drawing, or from the top right for left-handers.

Short, sharp marks drawn from the thumb and forefinger:

Longer, curved marks drawn from the wrist:

Long, sweeping marks drawn from the elbow:

Line

Although lines do exist in the visual world they often represent an idea that we impose rather than something that we can actually see. A line is a good way of translating and simplifying complex visual information by "standing in" to represent a boundary of some kind.

Drawing a Line

A line can be beautiful—a single, virtuous mark that tells a flowing tale about the contours of the subject. It can be straight and solid, smooth and curving; it can zigzag to and fro on the page. The beginner will often spend too long staring at the line as they draw, making little feathery marks. Be confident in drawing a line: work out where it will start and stop, and then with your eye on your model and glancing down to the page occasionally, pull the line through the drawing in a continuous mark that describes the boundary that you see. If you're not happy with where the line lies, rub it out lightly and redraw it again with confidence.

A hesitant beginner's line:

A line made with the tip of a sharp pencil, and lines made with the side of a blunt pencil:

Weight of Line

Experiment with the weight you can put behind your pencil, and see how this affects the line. A heavy line can be good for suggesting areas of shadow, while a light line can be used for brighter parts of the figure. Variety of line weight in a drawing will keep it dynamic.

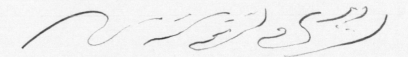

Tone

What is Tone?

Sometimes line doesn't provide enough information about the subject, and you'll want to represent the visual world as you actually see it, through graduations of light and dark. That is where tone can become part of your drawing vocabulary. Think of tone as the grayscale you'd get if you turned your model black and white. It is not the same as color, although colors have tone; yellows, for example, are often tonally lighter than blues. To understand the tone of a color, think about how it might look if it was photocopied in black and white.

Why Is Tone Helpful in a Drawing?

Although the outline of the face can describe the overall shape of the subject, there are more shapes within the outline that are sculpted by the light that falls on them. We see all things by the reflection of light; shadow is created by the interruption of light by a form. It is through shadows and highlights that we see the world and so truly understand the form of the face. A purely linear drawing can appear flat; by drawing selective shadows into the subject you can add depth to a linear study.

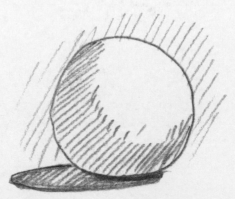

Tonal Range

Everything you see has a tonal value, and the materials you are using will set the tonal range possible in your drawing. The darkest dark you'll be able to achieve, representing the pencil pressed hard against the page, is at one end of the scale. The lightest light is the white of the paper and sits at the other end. Different pencils will give different tonal ranges, so a 9B will allow you to achieve a very dark tone, while a 4H will give a narrower tonal range, but will allow you more subtlety when trying to achieve the light tones. Experiment with your materials to work out the ranges of your pencils.

Tonal gradients made with the side of a pencil:

Tonal gradients showing the different tonal ranges of 4H, HB, and 6B pencils:

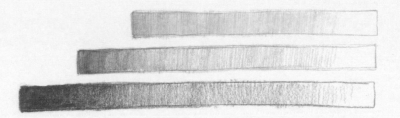

If you're aiming for realistic representation, then don't be heavy-handed with your tone; save the darkest mark your pencil can make for the darkest shadow you can see and the white of your paper for the very brightest highlight. Everything thing else will be a mid-tone. It's a common mistake to make drawings too high-contrast. Start to look for the highlights you get within shadows and vice versa, or, to get an overall impression of tone, unfocus your eyes a little.

Tonal Vocabulary

Before you go shading your drawings, it is a good idea to develop some tonal mark-making. Lines that are packed closely together on the page can be used to represent tone, as can smooth "shaded" graduations of light to dark. Consistent mark-making when drawing tone will stop your shadows being mistaken as texture. Scribbly lines moving in different directions are hard to control, awkward to put down, and difficult for the viewer to read as tone. Here are some examples of tonal mark-making to try out:

Swift, parallel marks are quick to draw and give consistent tone. Explore crosshatching: crisscross the lines to make diamonds rather than making grids as it is more sympathetic to curved surfaces like skin.

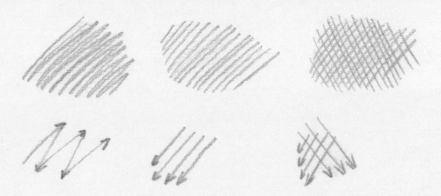

Don't be afraid to go over the edges of a line; it is better to retain energy in the marks than to keep them within the boundaries. The tone can always be cleaned up with an eraser later.

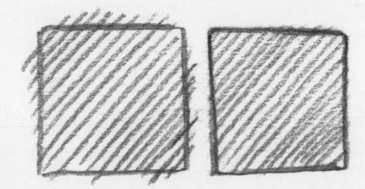

Light

When you draw shadow, you are really drawing the effects of light on your subject; sometimes you'll need to draw light back in after darkening an area. This is where your eraser can become a tool for drawing.

INITIAL LINE DRAWING:

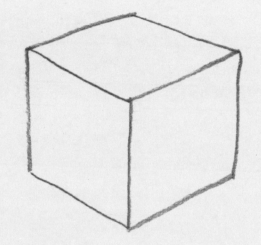

TONE ADDED:

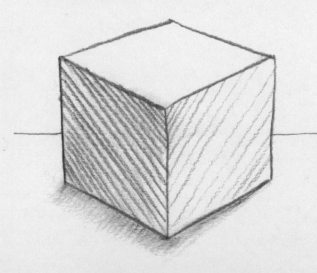

To enhance the illusions of light, you'll want to strengthen the contrasts at the boundaries. Where a dark surface meets a light surface, make the dark edge darker and the light edge lighter. Explore how you can use your eraser as a tool to draw light, and cut your eraser at an angle to get a sharp edge. Note: if you're working on white paper, chalk won't make a dark area lighter; at best, it will bring it back to the paper color, but it will often just mix with the dark medium to make gray. White media works much better on colored or off-white paper.

ERASER USED TO INCREASE CONTRAST AT BORDERS:

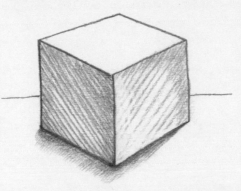

Use tone in the background to push highlighted areas forward. Look at your subject and background to work out which is lighter and add tone to bring out the contrast. Background tone doesn't need to be constant but can change to serve the subject.

BACKGROUND SHADED TO MAKE SUBJECT STAND OUT:

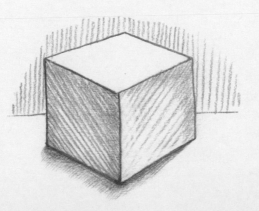

Observational Measuring

When people talk about measuring in drawing, they don't mean using a ruler. Observational measuring is about learning to estimate proportions by eye and translating them across to your drawings. Your ability to measure between points and judge the shapes of things you see will improve with experience. The ideal isn't to always use tools and shortcuts to help you but to train your eye so that eventually you will be able to measure without thinking about it. Sometimes you might need a few tricks to help you out, so here are some techniques to try.

Measuring with a Pencil

When a distance in the subject is difficult to estimate, you might find it helpful to use your pencil to measure. Hold your pencil at arm's length, close one eye (to flatten what you see), and put the top of the pencil against one side of the thing you want to measure. Slide your thumb along to the other side. You then have a distance "measured out" that you can translate across to other parts of the subject, allowing you to compare one length to another. This all makes you look super arty, but don't get carried away; it is best to use this approach for checking tricky proportions rather for all your measuring.

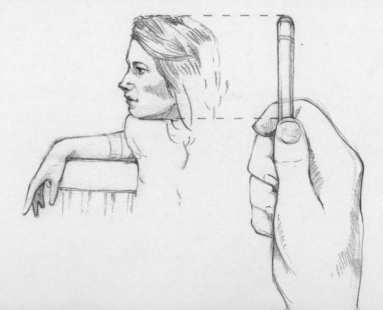

Verticals, Horizontals, and Diagonals

Many problems can be solved in drawings by checking vertical and horizontal relationships. Hold your pencil in the same ways as described for measuring (a plumb line can also be used), and line it up with one part of your drawing. By keeping the pencil level and running your eye along it you can check which other parts of the subject should be directly below or above your fixed point. If it doesn't line up in the same way in your drawing, then you know something has gone awry. You can also hold the pencil at an angle to check diagonals in the body and quickly translate them across to your drawing.

Viewfinders

A viewfinder can also help you check horizontals and verticals. It blocks out confusing information around your subject and can help you compose a drawing. To make one, just cut a window the shape of your paper in a piece of cardboard, and then hold it up between your eye and the subject to isolate your model.

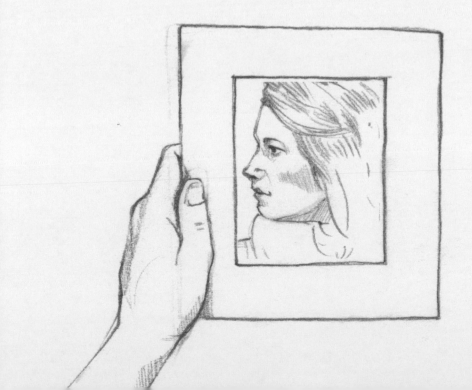

The Technique

In this section I've broken the drawing process down into three broad stages with a fourth stage of "understanding" that runs parallel to them all. It is a classical approach to drawing, working from the inside features of the face and spiraling out. Erasing is encouraged between stages—not to erase what you've done, but to push your marks back to make way for the next layer.

A Beginner's Approach

The first stage, establishing the shape, can be the most difficult for beginners as it relies on a certain level of understanding and draftsmanship. Although it is the ideal way to start, you might find it easier to skip straight to the second stage, construction. As you advance as a draftsman, revisit these early instructions to see if you can gain a better appreciation of them with experience.

Start Simple

Try drawing something simple first to avoid getting bogged down in the detail of the face. A solid natural form like a skull, or a piece of fruit, would be ideal; I've used an apple as an example.

STAGE 1:

ESTABLISHING THE FORM

This drawing establishes the basic shapes of the subject on the page, as well as roughly setting the scale and size of the drawing. It will give you a starting point, a chance to exercise your observation skills and compose the drawing so that it fits on the page.

1: LOOK

First look at your subject for five to ten seconds. Let your pencil hover over your paper. See how your subject sits in its surroundings, think about it, and try to really see it. Look for the edges of the shape, the lights, darks, textures, and shadows.

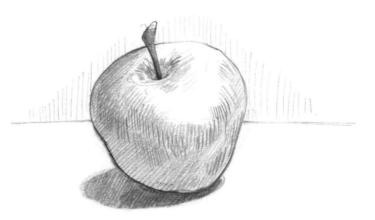

2: ESTABLISH

After a few moments of looking, jot out some intuitive marks that feel around the form of the subject. Feel your way around the subject loosely and quickly with your eyes, and sketch the form on the page as you look. Work fast, aiming for five to ten seconds of drawing.

PARALLEL STAGE: UNDERSTANDING

All the while that you draw, you want to have
some idea of the nature of the thing you are drawing.
Drawing reinforces this understanding; the more you
draw something, the better you understand it and the
better you'll draw it next time. The cross section of the
apple can help your understand its shape, and the
line of the table can help you understand its position.
Knowing the direction of light will help you understand
the shadow it casts.

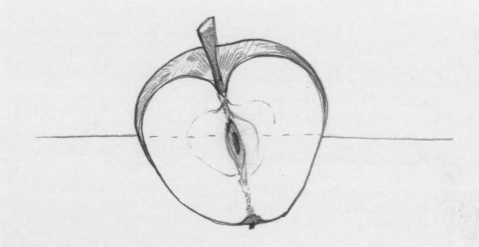

STAGE 2:

CONSTRUCTING THE SHAPE

At this stage, you are looking to correct and firm up the
shapes established in the first drawing. Before getting
carried away with details, look for simple geometric
shapes in your subject. Identify a few key features to use
as landmarks and build in some simple lines to map out
the relationships between those points. Base these lines
on what you really see rather than what you expect to
see, and draw them in intuitively.

1: ERASE

Lightly erase the establishing drawing, leaving some of it showing through.

2: ESTABLISH

Jot in the limits of the shape and its relationship to the background.

3: CONSTRUCT

Draw in any important shapes underpinning the subject and identify any important landmarks.

STAGE 3:

ELABORATING ON THE DRAWING

This final stage is still an editing stage, where the previous drawing is refined further. Elaborating on the drawing can mean many things. You may want to keep the drawing simple and linear, and so spend your time strengthening the outline of the shape and key features. Or you may want to delve into tone, mapping the shadows on the subject and background. I'll touch on both here, but there are many ends in the drawing that can be pursued.

1: LIGHTLY ERASE

Lightly erase the construction lines, leaving some showing through.

2: ADD LINE

Using the construction lines as a scaffold for your drawing, you can start to describe the inner and outer lines that shape the subject. Don't be afraid to reassess and change proportions as you go, but try to keep one point or construction line constant so that you can always refer back to that point when checking measurements. Play around with the weight of line as you draw, pressing heavier where there are shadows.

3: ADD TONE

Add tone and shadow to the subject; be selective and pick out as much or as little shadow as you think is important.

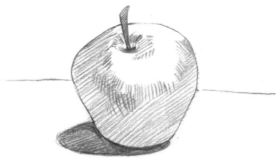

4: DEFINE

Use your eraser to clean up the tone and draw in light, and use your pencil to darken shadows and redefine key lines.

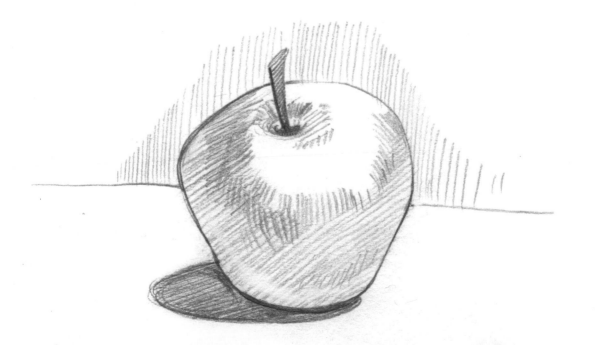

THE BASIC PORTRAIT SKETCH

The approach in this book relies on layering one drawing over another. The first layer is the basic portrait sketch, a quick sketch that lays the foundation for later, more developed drawing. This sketch can be an end in itself, particularly if you're sketching out and about. If you're clever in your drawn selections, the less you put into a drawing the more accurate it can appear, as the viewer is left to fill in the gaps. The longer you spend on a drawing, the more accurate you have to be to make it convincing. Practice this quick technique as often as you can and develop the approach presented in this chapter to suit your own needs. Set a time limit of five minutes or so for each drawing.

This chapter builds directly on the attitudes and techniques explained in the previous one, so to get the most from it you'll need to have read that first. When you're drawing the face, bear in mind that you're really drawing the head; it is a three-dimensional object connected to the rest of the body, not just an arrangement of features.

A Visual Conversation

When you draw a portrait, think of the process as similar to meeting someone for the first time. At first, you take in their overall shape and appearance, then you might engage with their eyes, and next move your gaze around the rest of their face taking in their changing expressions. By following a similar approach in your drawings (impression to eyes to features) you follow a familiar and rehearsed way of seeing the face. By creating the right emphasis in your portrait drawings, you can pull the viewer into your pictures in the same way.

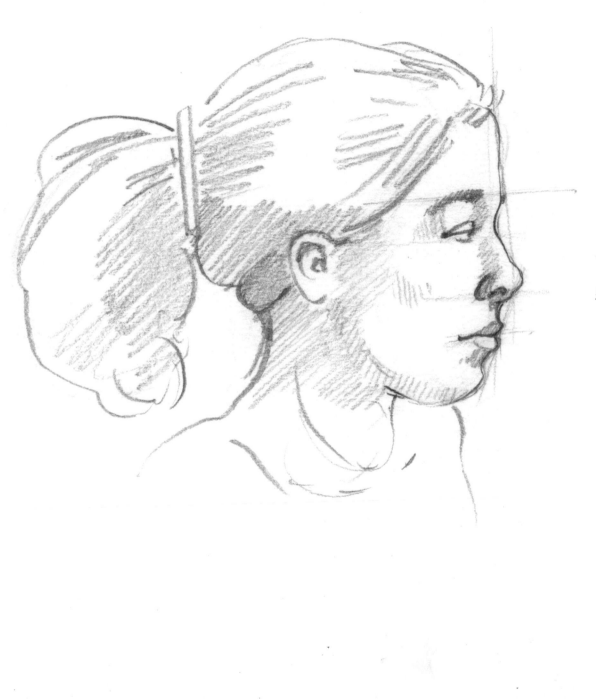

Stage 1: Establishing the Head

First, look at your subject for five to ten seconds. Let your pencil hover over the paper. Think about what you want to communicate about your sitter and try to understand what it is that feels engaging about their face.

Then, make quick marks for the top of the head, bottom of the chin, and left and right limits of the face. Sketch in marks for the neck and shoulders and start placing the shadows that mark out the eyes, nose, and mouth quickly and loosely and with a continuous, fast, flowing line. You are trying to see your way around the face with your pencil in the same way a blind sculptor might feel his way around the face of his subject. Work quickly, aiming for a five to ten second drawing.

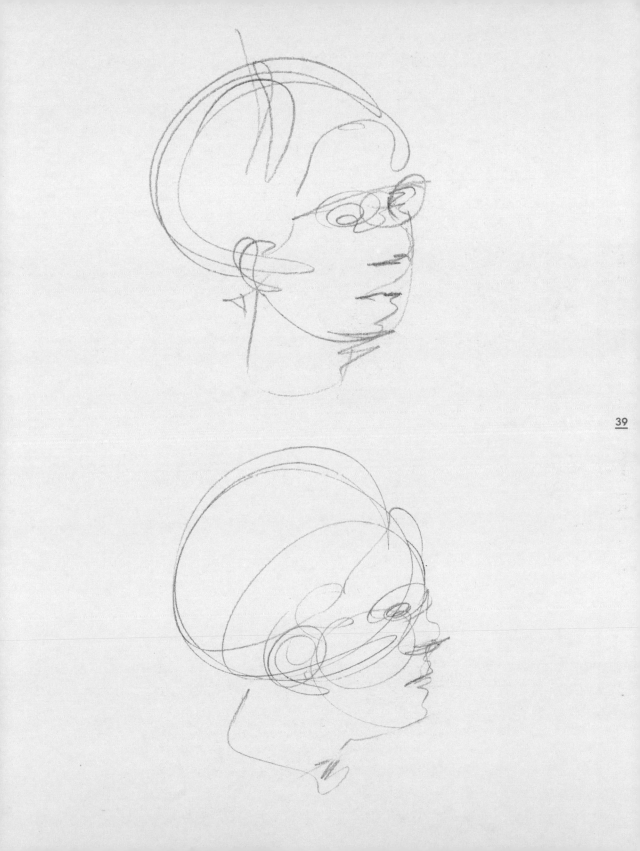

39

Understanding the Head

A basic understanding of anatomy should always underpin
your drawings. The face is the surface expression of what
is going on underneath the skin. You can often understand
a face and head better when you think about how the skull
looks underneath it. Here are a few anatomical details to
look out for in the head. If there is something proportionally
wrong about your drawing, think about how it would look
with a skull drawn over it so that you can identify problems
with the underlying structure.

Think about:
a) The shape of the eye socket.
b) The shape and position of the cheekbones.
c) The shape of the jaw.
d) The placing of the spine.
e) The size of the back of the skull.

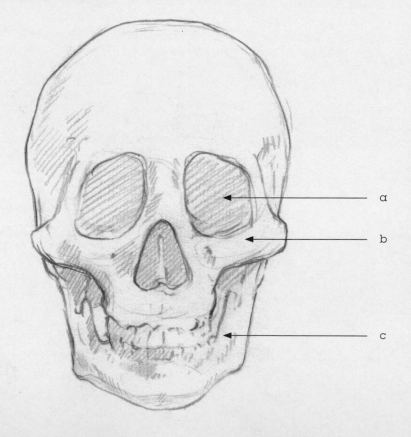

a

b

c

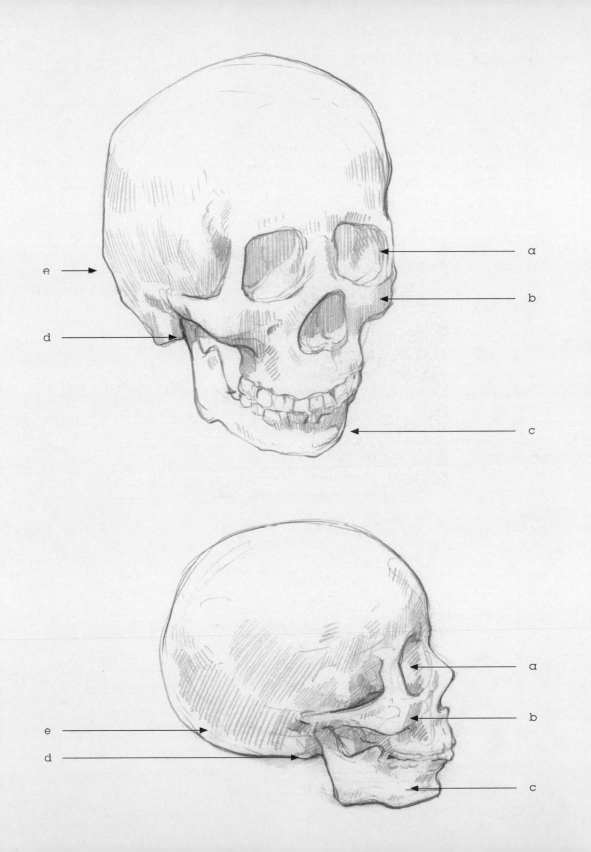

a

b

c

e

d

a

b

e

d

c

Stage 2: Constructing the Head

Use your eraser to rub your first "establishing sketch" back so that faint marks remain visible. You'll now want to add in some guidelines for drawing the head; be prepared to move these lines around as you check and reassess the proportions of the face. First jot in a quick line across the eyebrows—all your following lines will "hang" from this first eyebrow line, so treat it as a "safe point" that remains fixed. Work from that eyebrow line downwards, dashing in the key proportions of the face. Change and move these lines in relation to the eyebrow line until you are happy that they represent the spacing of facial features as you see them.

Look for these hanging lines:
a) The eyebrow line from the far edge of one eyebrow to the far edge of the other.
b) The line across the eyes from the far corner of each eye.
c) The underside of the nose where the nose meets the philtrum.
d) The centerline of the lips from one edge of lip to the other.

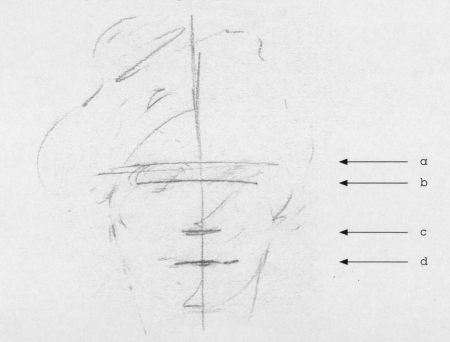

a

b

c

d

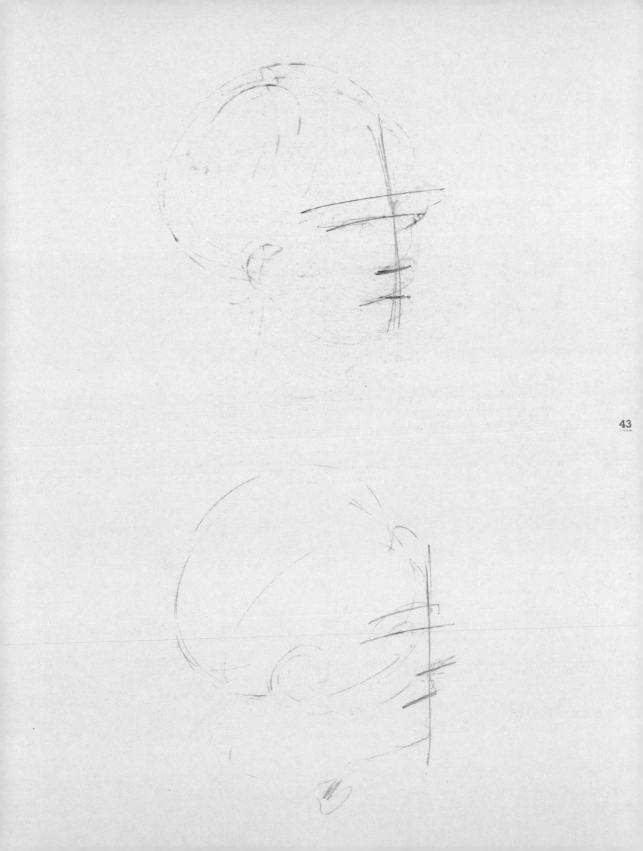

Further Construction

Once you reach the lips, move down to the chin. It is easy to underestimate the space here, so check it twice! From the chin you can trace a line taking you up the jaw to the ears—think about the shape of the skull as you do this. Mark the limits of the ear and continue your line up around the forehead and hairline. At the same time, look at the triangle you get between the edges of the eyes and the bottom of the nose. Check the relationship between these points by jotting the triangle in.

Look for these lines and points:
a) The bottom of the chin.
b) The line of the jaw, looking at where it changes direction as it moves up the cheek.
c) The limits of the ear, comparing the position of the ear to the features (it should sit between the eye and the bottom of the nose).
d) The hairline, and the outside limit of the hair.

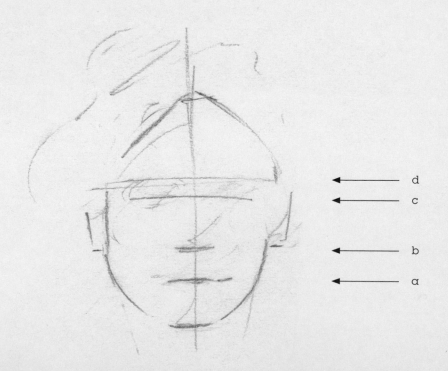

d

c

b

a

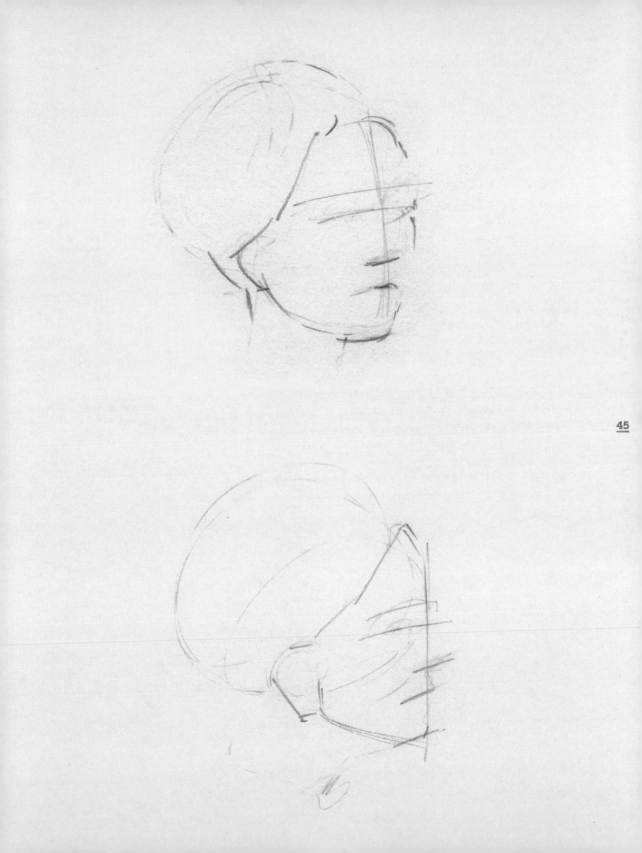

Stage 3: Elaborating on the Head

Thus far, you've established the head in Stage 1 and constructed it in more detail in Stage 2. Use an eraser to rub back your construction lines so that they are just visible; you are now ready for Stage 3, and can use the faint lines as a scaffold for building up the face. Again, work from the eyebrows down and develop a shorthand vocabulary for the features.

Here's where the face starts to look more like a face. Keep the features simple (after all, you don't have much time for this quick sketch) and pay as much attention to the space between the features as you do to the features themselves. If they look out of line with one another, don't be afraid to change them. A beginner's error is to draw cartoon-like "symbolic" features rather than drawing what is observed. If you're working with a dark medium on light paper, you should be drawing things on the face that are dark, letting the white paper be the light areas; by drawing the dark lines and shadows that make up what your see of the face, you'll be able to create the illusion of the face on the paper.

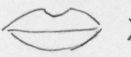 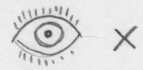

1: EYEBROWS

There can be huge range in the shape, weight, and expression of the eyebrows. Observe them carefully and block the eyebrows in simply.

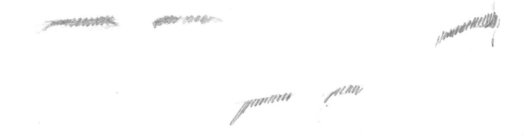

2: EYES

The eyelashes are dark and the iris and pupil are both dark from a distance, so block those in as one, leaving a highlight for the under-eyelid.

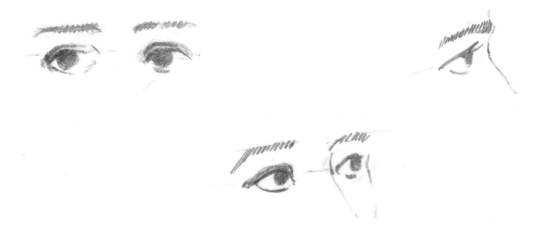

3: **NOSE**

Draw in the nostrils and the shadow underneath the nose to suggest its shape—the full line of the nose is only needed when the head is turned.

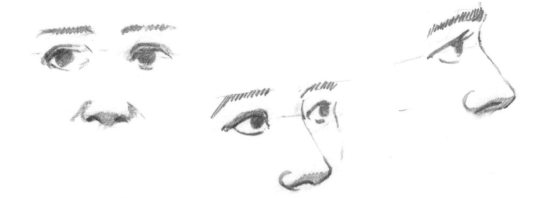

4: **MOUTH**

Use the shadow of the philtrum under the nose to take you down to the lips. It is the centerline of the lips that is most important, so put that in first. Block in shadows in the top lip; the bottom lip is best shaped using the shadow underneath.

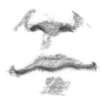
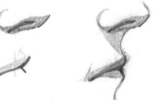

5: CHIN

Don't underestimate the size of the chin; use the shadow below the lip to take you to the ball of the chin and then move back up to the jaw.

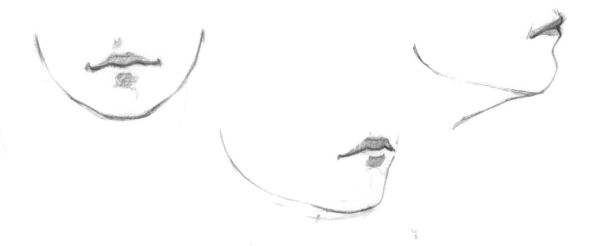

6: EAR

Keep the ear simple—look at the space it fills and outline it. If you want more detail, look for these lines in it.

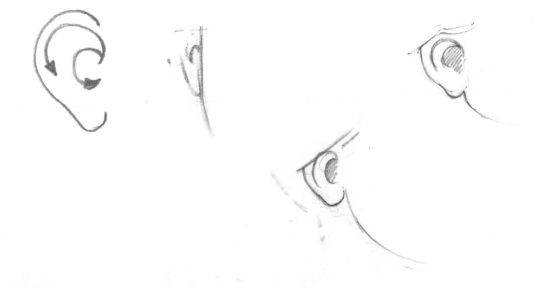

Here's how to put all that together.

As you're putting the features onto the face, selectively use tone to pick out key shadows, look for the shape of the shadows, and use them to bridge the spaces between features.

Shaping the Hair

There can be a tendency in beginners to try to draw the hair as lots of individual lines on top of a bald head, but it is often much better to understand the hair as one big mass that is part of the head's shape. Draw the borders of the hair as an outline as if it were a hat more than hair.

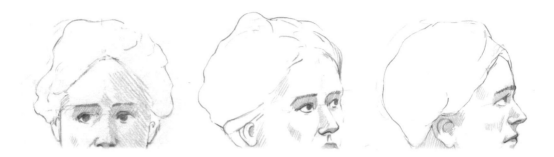

1: <u>FLOW</u>

Look for "flows" in the hair, big movements of hair that you can use to break up and add detail to the overall mass.

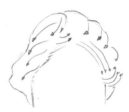

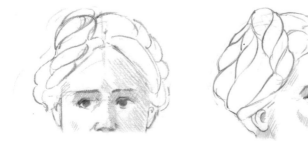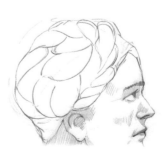

2 : TONE

Block in tone in the direction that the hair flows using quick, clear marks (see tone and shadow in Chapter 2). Look at how dark the hair actually is compared to the face.

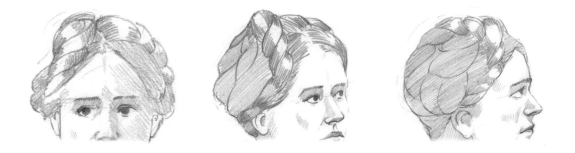

3 : TEXTURE

To add character, bring further marks into the hair to represent texture. Take a look at the later section on hair (p. 92) for more advice.

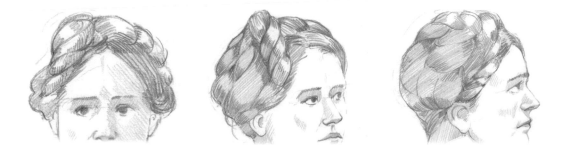

Checking Relationships

The reevaluation of features is as important as the initial measurements. Don't be afraid to alter your drawing; in fact, don't be afraid to erase most of it in order to shift all the features a little bit this way or that. If you are unhappy with the proportions of the drawing, it is always better to erase parts of it back and then redraw them rather than try to preserve bits of the drawing that you're happy with. Once you've drawn most or all of the features, sit back, hold your drawing out, compare it to your sitter, and decide what changes may need to be made. Then make them.

Here are a few important things to look out for. The dotted lines don't need to be drawn in, but should be thought about as you draw. Despite common patterns in all faces, these relationships will vary depending on the model and their position in relation to you.

a) Eye to nose triangle.
b) Nose to mouth rhombus.
c) Vertical relationships.
d) Horizontal relationships.

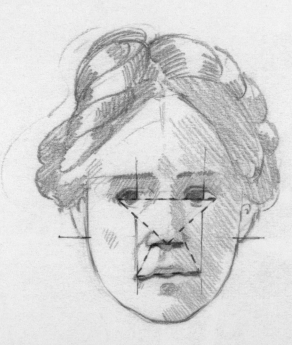
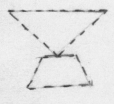

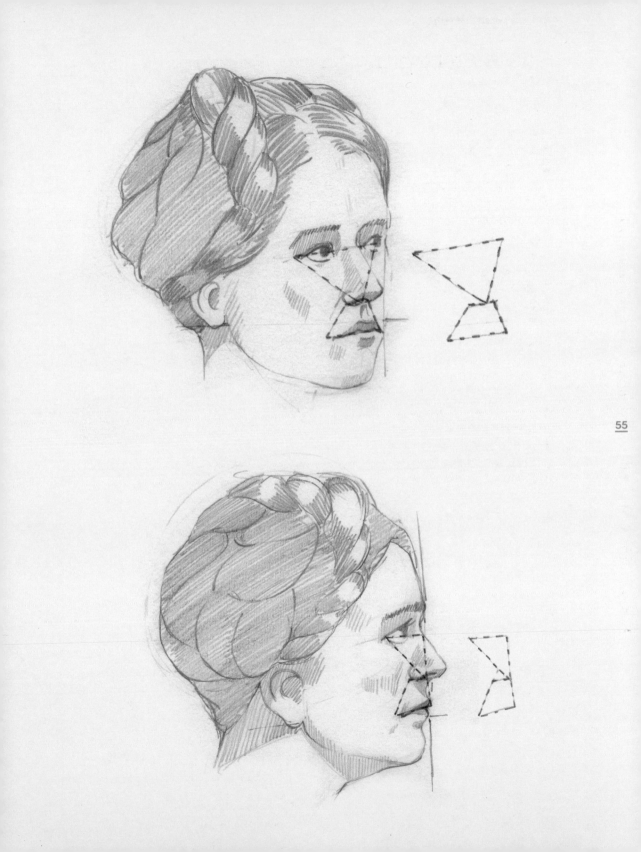

Putting It All Together

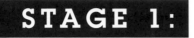

STAGE 1:

ESTABLISHING

1: <u>LOOK</u>

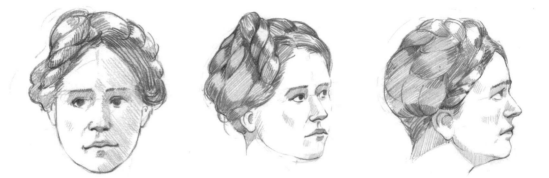

2: <u>ESTABLISH</u>

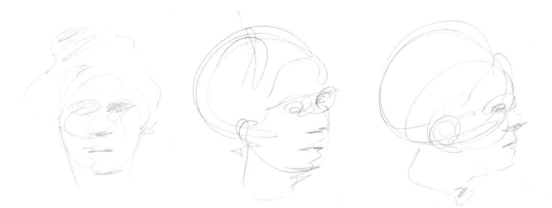

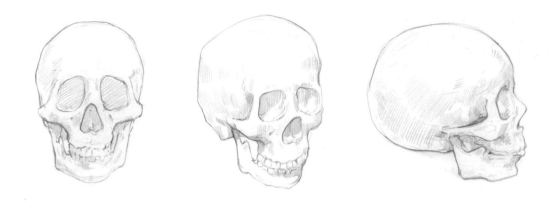

STAGE 2:

CONSTRUCTING

1: ERASE BACK

2: <u>CONSTRUCT FEATURES</u>

3: <u>CONSTRUCT OUTLINE</u>

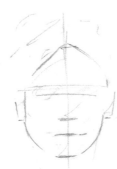 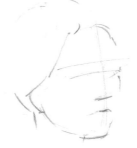 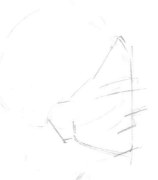

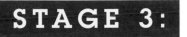

STAGE 3:

ELABORATING

1: ERASE BACK

2: ELABORATE ON FEATURES

3: ELABORATE ON OUTLINE AND TONE

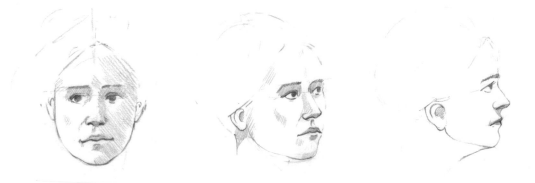

4: ELABORATE ON HAIR

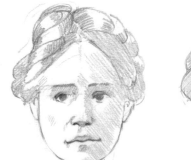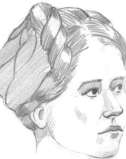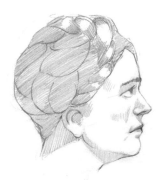

5: CHECK RELATIONSHIPS

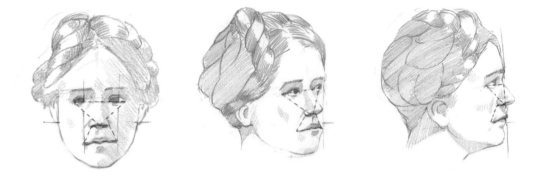

6: ALTER IF NEEDED

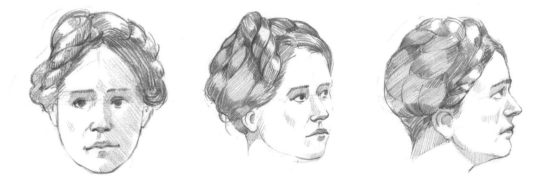

Understanding the Head and Shoulders

The head is rarely drawn in isolation, but will often be set in the context of the neck and shoulders. The neck is much bigger than is often anticipated as it's a huge, complex pillar of muscle, bone, and piping that supports the whole head, not a thin tube that sits on the shoulders. Much of the anatomical underpinning of the neck and shoulders is very close to the surface of the skin, and it can really help to understand what is going on around there in order to draw it well.

Avoid drawing the neck like this:

Try drawing it more like this:

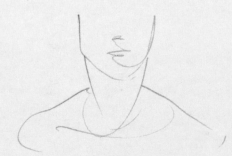

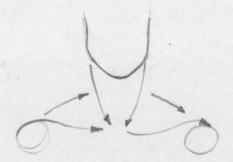

Look at this: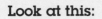

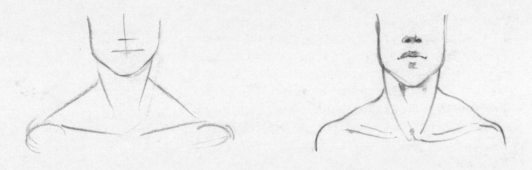

And understand this a little better:

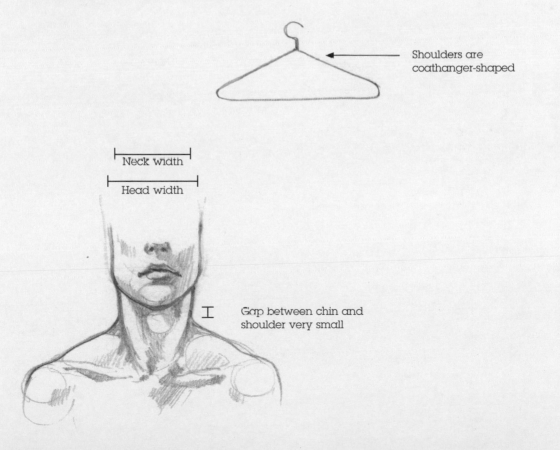

Shoulders are
coathanger-shaped

Neck width

Head width

Gap between chin and
shoulder very small

Understanding the Angles of the Head

If you are drawing somebody in a portrait sitting, you can ask them to change the angle of their head to get the view you want. In most natural situations, however, the head won't be held in the profile, front on, or three-quarter profile positions. Becoming a good portraitist means being able to understand and draw the head in all potential orientations. As the head moves up and down or side-to-side, relationships between the features change; the key to drawing the head lies in understanding these changes. Building on the basic portrait sketch, here are some general examples of how relationships change as the head moves.

Turn

As the head turns, one side of the face will slip away as the other side becomes larger; the curve of the back of the head (behind the ear) will also begin to appear.

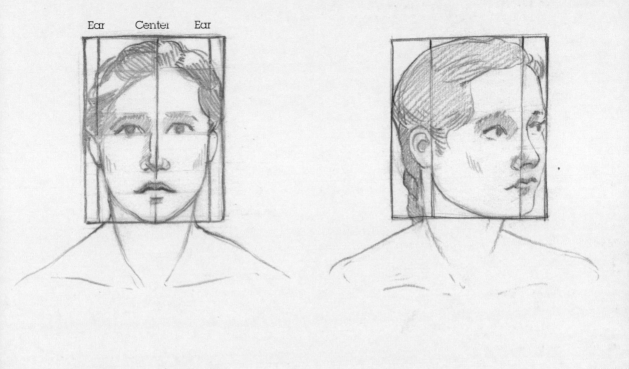

Ear   Center   Ear

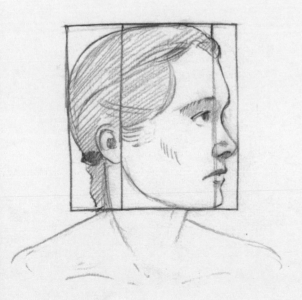

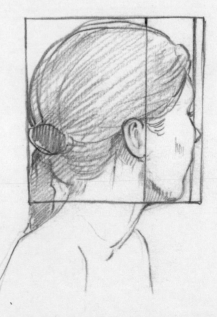

Tilt

As the head tilts back, the features of the face become compacted together—the hairline and forehead disappear and the undersides of the jaw and the nose become prominent. The neck becomes more visible, while the ears move very little, and the underside of the top lip becomes prominent and appears to curve down.

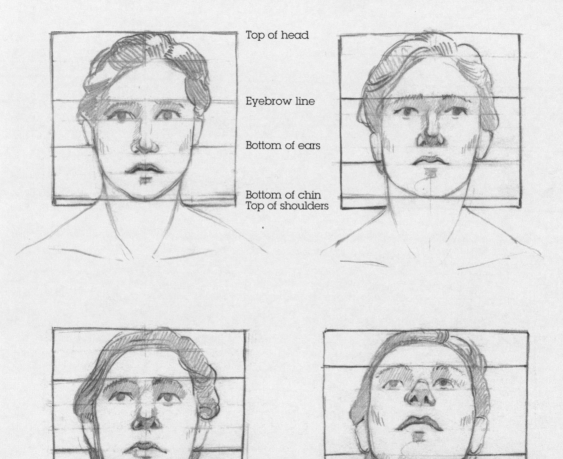

Top of head

Eyebrow line

Bottom of ears

Bottom of chin
Top of shoulders

As the head tilts forward, the features of the face once again become compacted together—the hairline, forehead, and the top of the nose become more prominent.

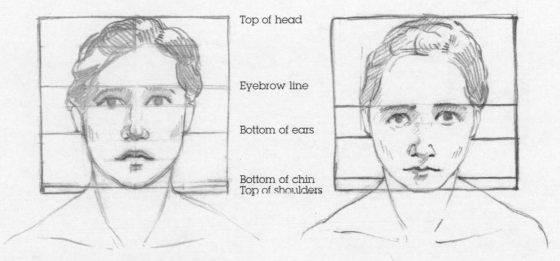

Top of head

Eyebrow line

Bottom of ears

Bottom of chin
Top of shoulders

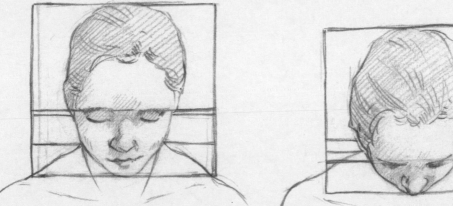

Negative Spaces

Negative space is the space around the figure. Drawing the negative space around the head can often be a good way to solve difficult problems.

When the angle of the head involves a turn and a tilt, you'll need to combine all of the previous understandings with further careful observation. It may help to have a look at the negative space between the head, neck, and shoulders.

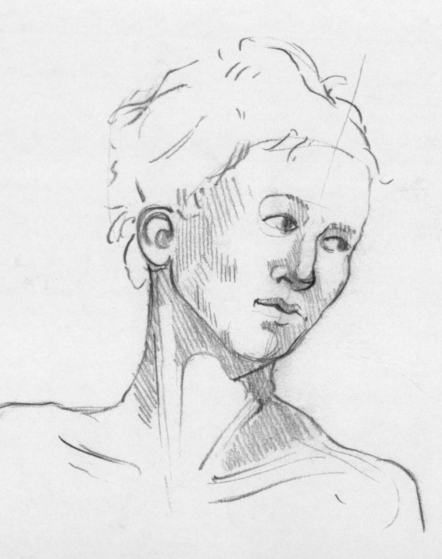

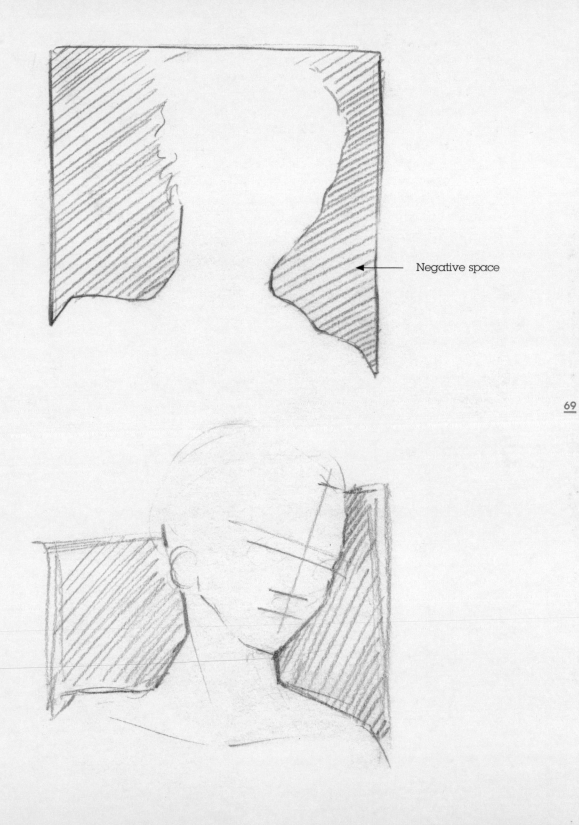

Negative space

Developing the Portrait

The following sections are intended as spotlights on the features. The likelihood is that through drawing portrait sketches you'll have already started to develop your own ways of dealing with the features in more detail. You can use these spotlights as a way of identifying and dealing with problems in your own drawings and solving the visual puzzles that you come across.

When drawing the face you'll need to keep panning back, looking at the drawing as a whole and then zooming in again on detail. Don't get too carried away working on one feature at a time. The spaces between the features are as important as the features themselves and if you are having a problem with how the face looks as a whole, it may be down to the relationships between features as much as the features themselves. Use the basic portrait sketch as a foundation and as always, take these techniques as a starting point, not as a substitute for your own observations.

Tone and Line

Tone and line are used together in all of these spotlights. As you work on more advanced portraits, use tone intelligently to say things about the surface of the face that line can't quite describe. Keep your mark-making simple and consistent, developing it as you become more confident. Think about experimenting with blocks of tone that follow the curve of the skin's surface.

A 15-minute portrait:

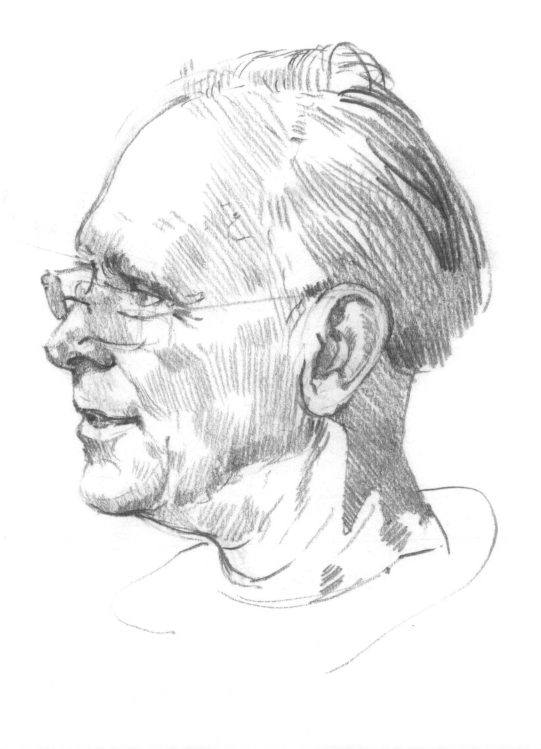

The Eyes

The eyes are typically the first thing that we settle on when looking at a drawing—absent eyes can lead to a lack of personality and engagement. Be careful that when drawing the pupils and irises, both the eyes are looking in the same direction.

Anatomy

The eyeball sits within the orbit of the skull. It is the skull's shape that creates the shadow around the eyes. The eyelids slide over the orb of the eye, and it's the round eyeball that helps shape the eyelids.

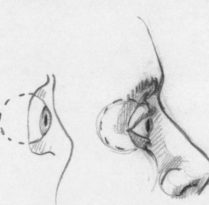 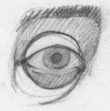

Problem Solving

Check that the spaces between the eyebrow and eyelid are correct and make sure that the eyes are spaced accurately, with an eye's-width between the two eyes.

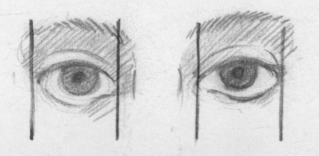

1: BASIC PORTRAIT SKETCH

2: ERASE BACK

3: CONSTRUCT

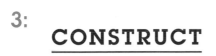 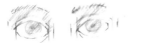

id="8" />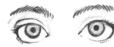

4: ELABORATE ON LINE

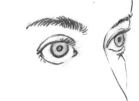

5: ELABORATE ON TONE

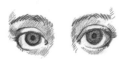 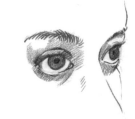

6: DRAW IN LIGHT WITH ERASER

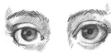 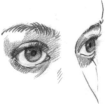

Eyes to Nose

When looking at the space between the eyes and nose, remember that the nose starts between the eyes, not underneath them. It is a common mistake to make the nose too long. Look at how close the shape of the eye socket is to the end of the nose.

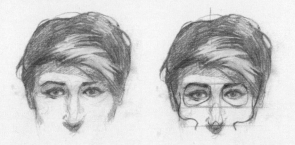

Look at the shape of the cheek bridging the gap between the eye and the top of the nostril. Try also to understand how the cheekbones sit in between the eyes and nose.

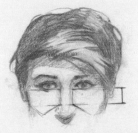

As the head turns, more of the side of the nose is revealed and this both obscures one eye and spaces the other eye further from the bridge of the nose. Look at how a single line appears to join the eyebrow to the nose.

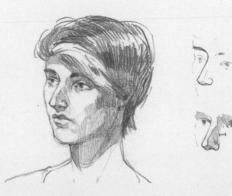

The Nose

The nose is the most sculptural part of the face, and to properly understand how to draw portraits you need an understanding of the nose from all angles. In profile the line of the nose will have the most impact on how you perceive it; from front on the size and shape of the nostrils will appear more important. You can best shape the nose from the front through good use of tone, and from the side with good use of line.

Anatomy
The skull shows how flat much of the face is without the protrusion of the nose; the cartilage of the nose brings it a long way out from the average line of the profile.

Problem Solving
Check the width of the nostrils against the eyes above, and check the triangle between the edges of the eyes and the bottom of the nose to make sure it is the right length. Make sure any tone in the nose reflects the shadow you actually see there; tone is often complex in the nose, as it is describing a complicated shape.

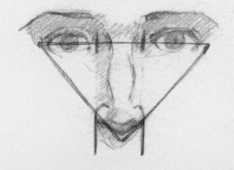

1: BASIC PORTRAIT SKETCH

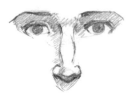 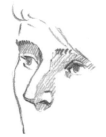 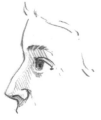

2: ERASE BACK

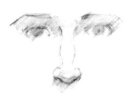  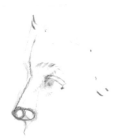

3: CONSTRUCT

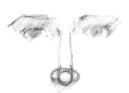 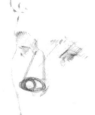 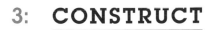

4: ELABORATE ON LINE

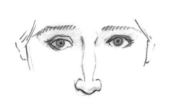
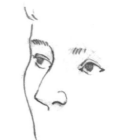

5: ELABORATE ON TONE

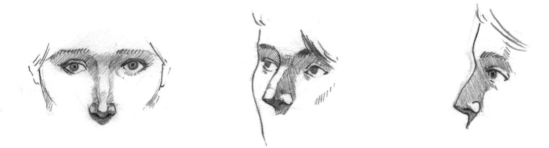

6: DRAW IN LIGHT WITH ERASER

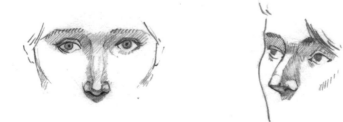
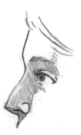

The Nose at Different Angles

At different angles the top or bottom of the nose can become more visible. Have a look at how the circle at the end of the nose changes in relationship to the oval of the nostrils.

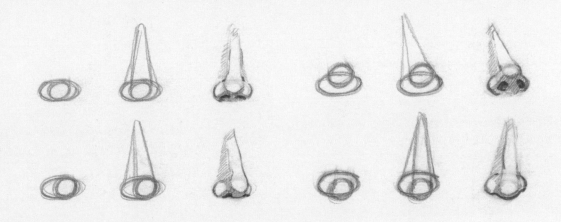

Nose to Mouth

The fleshy area above the top lip will help you understand the distance between the nose and mouth. The shape and depth of the philtrum will differ a lot from person to person. Check back up to the eyes as you move down to the lips to keep the whole face unified as one.

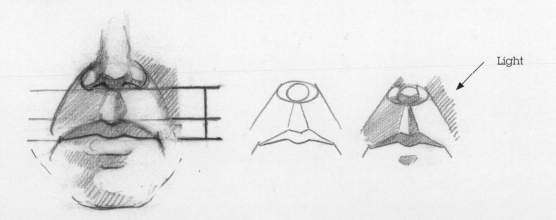

Light

The Mouth

The line of the lips is one of the most beautiful and articulate parts of the face and is the source of much of our expression of character, mood, thought, and emotion.

Anatomy

The mouth is surrounded by a doughnut of muscle that allows it to articulate movements, along with further muscles connected to this doughnut that tug on the corners of the lips. The mouth is a slit in the face with the lips turning outward where the opening of the mouth is at its widest.

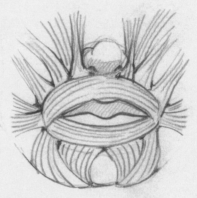

Problem Solving

Check that the line of the mouth begins and ends in the correct places, and that it is symmetrical (if indeed your model's mouth or expression is symmetrical). You should avoid outlining the lips heavily, although you can achieve fullness in the lips by finding ovals that underpin its shape. Look at the sharpness of the V where the two lips meet in a profile drawing.

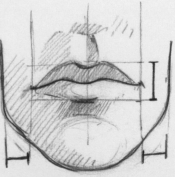

1: BASIC PORTRAIT SKETCH

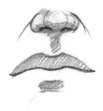 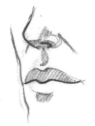 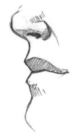

2: ERASE BACK

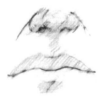 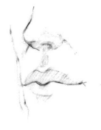 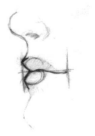

3: CONSTRUCT

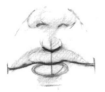 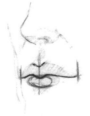 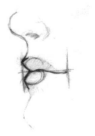

4: ELABORATE ON LINE

5: ELABORATE ON TONE

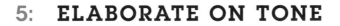

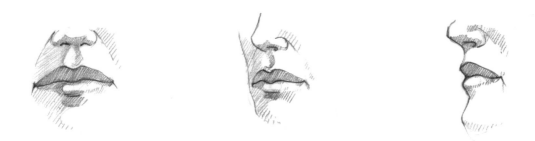

6: DRAW IN LIGHT WITH ERASER

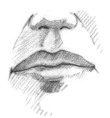

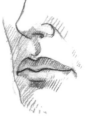

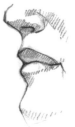

Teeth

When your model's teeth can be seen, either in a smile
or as part of the natural lay of their face, think about
how the lips are coming out over the shape of the skull.
See Expression (p. 100) for more on smiles.

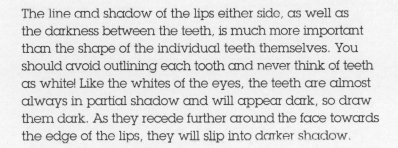

The line and shadow of the lips either side, as well as
the darkness between the teeth, is much more important
than the shape of the individual teeth themselves. You
should avoid outlining each tooth and never think of teeth
as white! Like the whites of the eyes, the teeth are almost
always in partial shadow and will appear dark, so draw
them dark. As they recede further around the face towards
the edge of the lips, they will slip into darker shadow.

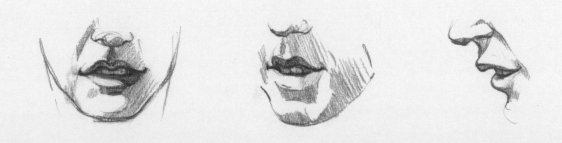

The Chin and Jaw

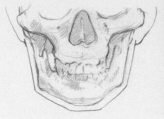

The jaw is the gateway from the head into the body and often serves as a foundation for the outline of the face.

Anatomy

To understand the size of the chin and the line taken by the jaw, think about the squareness of the jaw on a skull.

It is easy to underestimate the size of the chin, so measure the distance between the bottom of the lip and end of the chin and compare that to other parts of the face. Also, pay close attention to the size and shape of the shadows and highlights from bottom lip to chin to underside of the jaw. Depending on the lighting, it is easy to lose the line of the jaw; in profile, try emphasizing the beginning of the jaw near the ear and the curve of the jaw near the chin with a stronger line than you see.

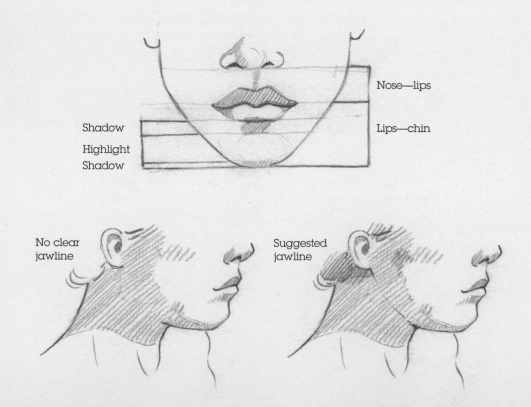

Nose—lips

Lips—chin

Shadow

Highlight

Shadow

No clear jawline

Suggested jawline

1: BASIC PORTRAIT SKETCH

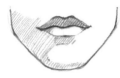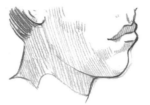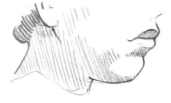

2: ERASE BACK

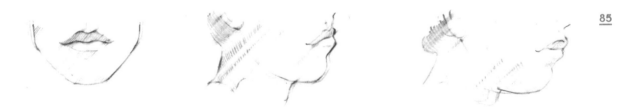

3: CONSTRUCT

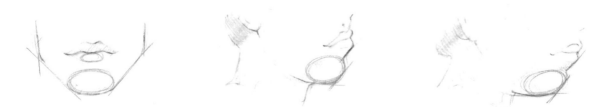

4: ELABORATE ON LINE

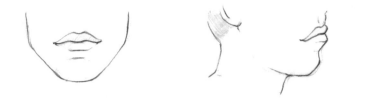

5: ELABORATE ON TONE

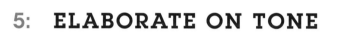

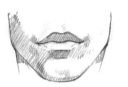
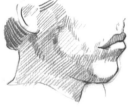
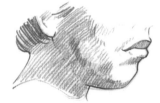

6: DRAW IN LIGHT WITH ERASER

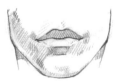
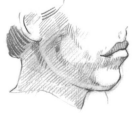
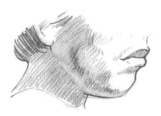

The Jaw and Neck

As the head tilts you'll see more or less of the jaw and neck. Think about the triangles and diamonds of shadow that the jaw opens up as it moves up and down.

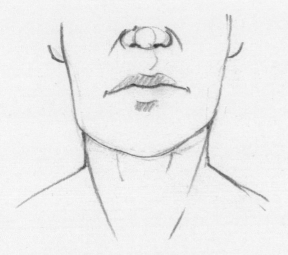

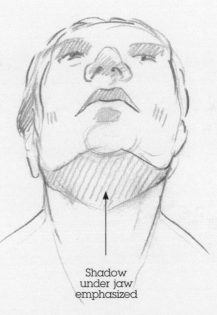

Shadow under jaw emphasized

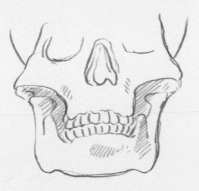

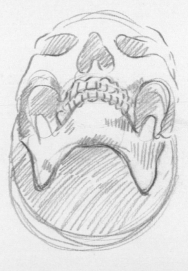

The Ears

Given its complex shape, the ear can cause a lot of stress for limited reward in a drawing, but diligent observation and a simple approach can often solve problems you may have.

Anatomy

The outer ear channels sound into the inner ear and its shape aids this, while protecting the inner ear from debris getting in. The ears sit close to the pivoting point of the head, so they move much less than other features as the head tips up and down; they are not used to signal expressions, so can be kept sketchier without weakening the portrait.

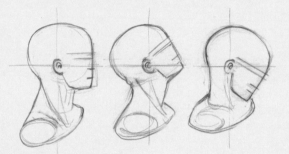

Problem Solving

Work out how important you feel the ear is in your drawing, and only draw it in as much detail as you need to—but make sure whatever you draw is based on observation. If you're going to leave it simple, just put a few lines in but follow the lines you actually see, don't just make do with a squiggle in the middle of the ear! If the head is turned or tilted, double-check the ears' positions in relation to other features.

1: BASIC PORTRAIT SKETCH

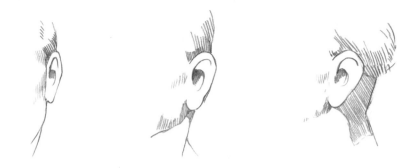

2: ERASE BACK

3: CONSTRUCT

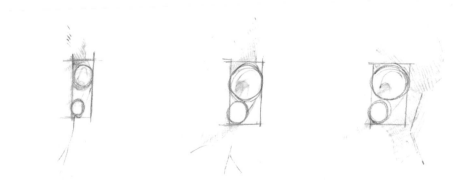

4: ELABORATE ON LINE

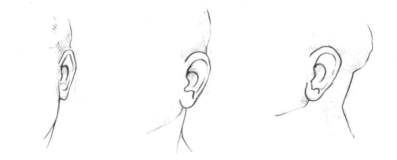

5: ELABORATE ON TONE

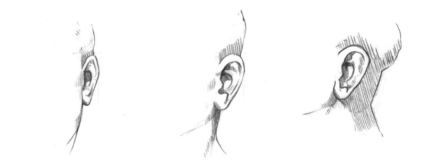

6: DRAW IN LIGHT WITH ERASER

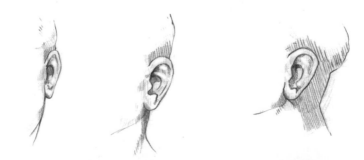

Differences in Ears

Ears differ hugely in shape; some have lobes, some do not, and although the structure remains consistent, it is fascinating to study individual differences. Earrings and jewelry can play an important part in your model's identity, so practice the simple blocks of light and dark that make up the reflective surface of a metal earring.

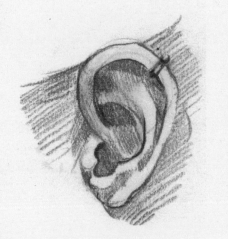

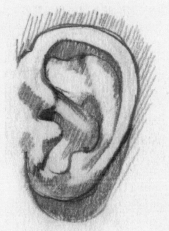

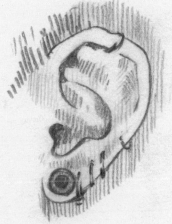

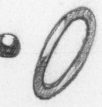

The Hair

Drawing Style

The hair is one of the best places to exercise personal expressions of artistic style. Just as any person might change their hair to alter their appearance, so the portraitist can change how the drawing is perceived by stylizing how the model's hair is drawn without having to alter their fundamental features. Be playful in how you deal with their hair—look at its outline, flow, and texture to understand it and make decisions about how you best want to deal with it.

Problem Solving

It is easy to get tone and texture mixed up when drawing the hair. Avoid drawing each hair individually from scalp to tip, and instead look at flows in the hair and use your marks to create an impression, communicating the tone and texture of what you see. To darken the hair, either use a tonal vocabulary that you've established elsewhere in the drawing or use marks indicating tone that move with the flow of the hair. You can use an eraser to bring in highlights. Here are some ways of dealing with different kinds of hair.

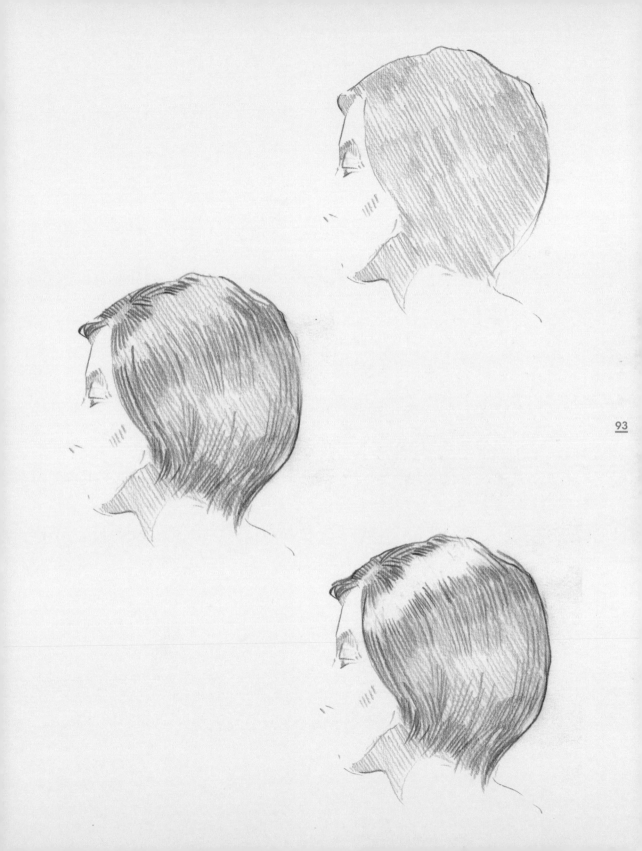

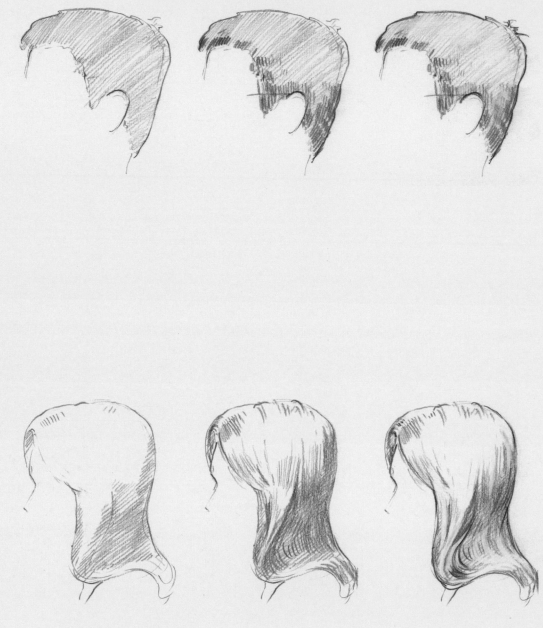

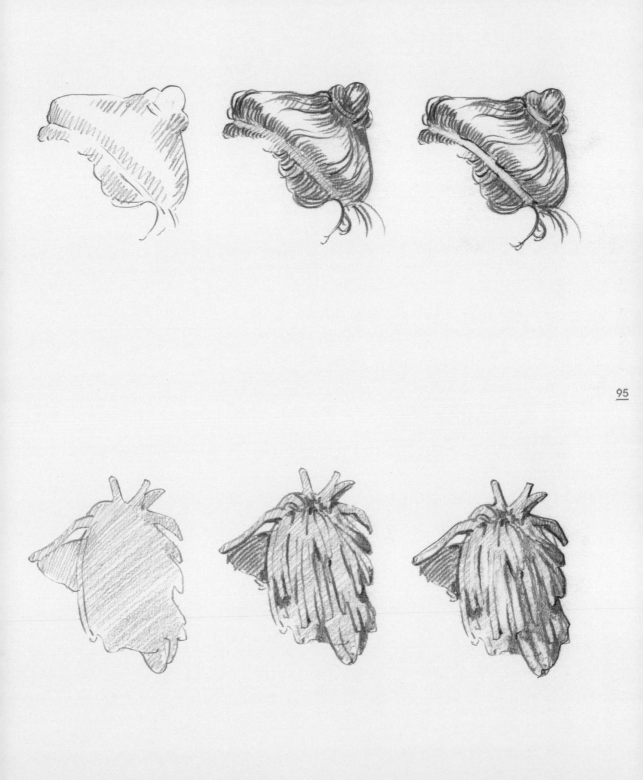

Facial Hair

Facial hair can be dealt with in much the same way
as hair on the head. If it is significant enough to have
its own mass on the face, then draw the outline in and
build up tone and texture in the same way. A big enough
moustache or beard can cast a shadow on the face, as
well as having its own tone. Stubble, which doesn't have
much mass itself, can be dealt with as if it were shadow
but with marks of texture that follow the directions of the
small hairs on the face.

Drawing of various styles of facial hair in different stages
of construction and elaboration:

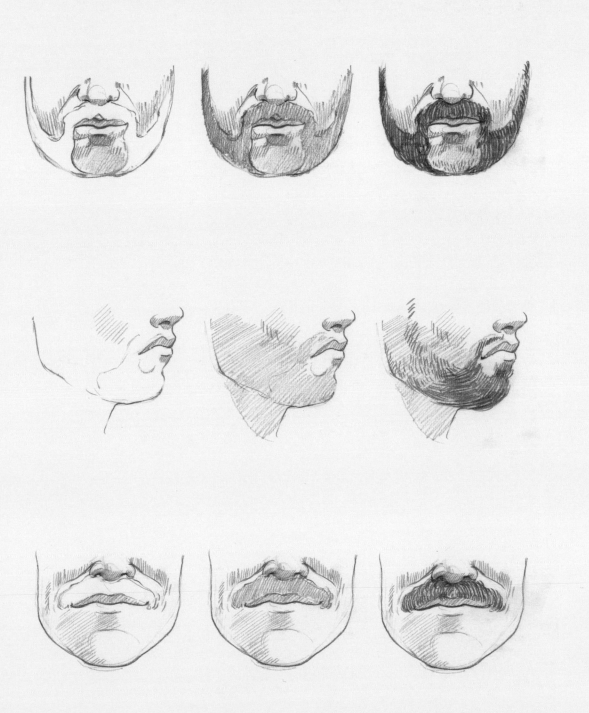

TAKING YOUR DRAWING FURTHER

Likeness

Likeness is an elusive thing. There are no hard and fast rules for getting a likeness in a drawing, but there are ways of increasing your chances of achieving one. It is often unhelpful to worry about likeness as you draw; sometimes you'll hit on it and sometimes you won't. Experience and proper observation are the key factors.

Emphasis

To understand how to create likeness, you need to understand what it is that makes someone's face unique. Work out what it is that interests you about your model's face and look at what it is that engages you about that part of them—is it the line of their nose? What shape is their nose when you really look? Then work out how you adapt your drawing to emphasize that characteristic and direct your drawing time accordingly. If it is their nose that's interesting, don't spend half your time drawing the ears; spend time observing and getting the nose just right. In this way, drawing a good likeness is partly making a face that measures up correctly to the face you see, but also partly caricature—that is, accentuating the things you find interesting.

The Articulate Face

It is important to understand that the face is an articulate thing, and a drawing is static by its nature. People's characters are particularly invested in the movements of their face, and when somebody sits for a portrait those movements will no longer be present. Try to study how your sitter's face moves when they speak and see if you can put any of the articulate nuances of their face into the drawing—for example, the lifting of cheeks or eyelids, twitches in the corner of the mouth, and so on.

Problem Solving

If your portrait seems to be falling short of a likeness, sit back and compare the drawing to the face you can see, and then return to the key features identified in the basic portrait. Look to see if you've accidently played down the shape of any of them, or misproportioned them, and alter your drawing accordingly. Here are a few examples of how to pull a drawing towards a better likeness.

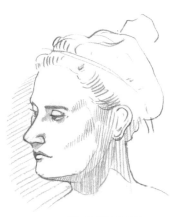

Weak likeness

To improve the likeness:

Avoid generic features

Include characterful details

Look at the specific shape of the eyebrow line,

the line of the nose,

and the center of the lips

Check the angle of the chin and jaw

Vary the weight of line in the outline to draw attention to important features

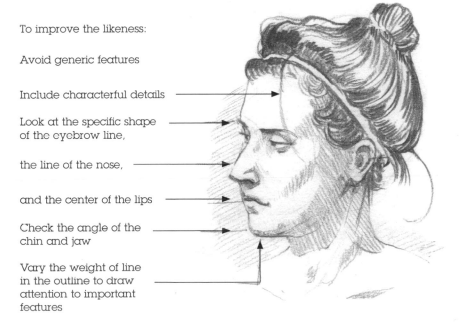

Strong likeness

Expression

Expression is a fleeting thing and is best captured fleetingly; quick sketches and intuitive drawings made in a few moments will often capture the most convincing expressions. If you want to capture particular expressions in a longer drawing, you'll have to be more tactical in how you approach it. Most people will relax into a "portrait" expression, which often translates as rather somber.

Capturing Expression

The best way to draw an expression is to build an understanding of what to expect so that you can capture it more easily when you see it. That way you will be able to draw the framework of the face from the relaxed expression of your sitter, and then when you see glimpses of the expression you want to achieve, you will know what to look out for and what to emphasize. You can jot out little visual "notes" that show how the face has changed slightly and elaborate on that using the information in the relaxed face. You can then capture more of the expression as you see it play over the face again and again. It is tricky, but the more you practice it the better you'll understand how the face works. Try practicing expressions in a mirror to get a feel for how your face moves. Opposite are some simple examples of expressions.

DRAWING FROM PHOTOS

Drawing expressions from photos will often lead to forced or wooden drawings, because you have no actual experience of how that person's face arrived at the expression or how they looked afterwards; this lack of understanding will translate into the drawing.

A SMILE

A smile is created by the contracting of facial muscles to pull the lips back over the teeth—look at how this changes the line of the lips and the shape of the cheeks as the muscles bunch up. Genuine smiles will also be accompanied by a widening of the eye and a lifting of the bottom eyelid.

A FROWN

A frown will be characterized by a narrowing of the eyes and pressing together of the lips, but primarily by the pulling down of the brow and the lowering of the eyebrow line.

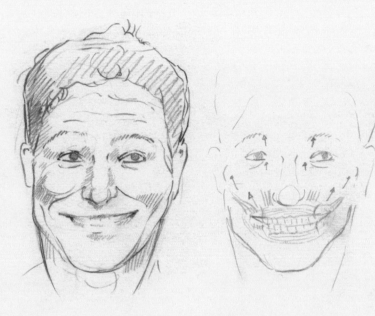

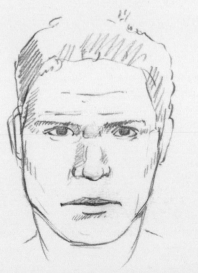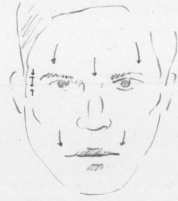

Age

Faces change over time; babies have a very different skull shape to adults and so the very structure of the head will alter as children age. The skull changes even further in old age. It is good to think about these underlying patterns in aging when drawing faces.

Babies

Babies have limited muscular control, so their faces will be soft and relaxed with a few major points of movement. Babies' skulls are longer, with a smaller jaw, but their eyes are about the same size as an adult, creating big proportional differences between a baby and an adult face.

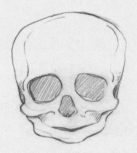 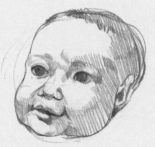

Children

As children grow, their skull shapes will move towards an adult shape. You can accentuate their smoother skin by being minimal with your tone and shading.

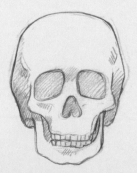 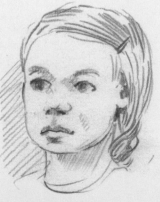

Elderly Faces

There are many characteristics of aging. Look for the creases and wrinkles that characterize an older face; they tell a lot about the expressions that the face is used to adopting, and expressions can be accentuated by exaggerating theses lines. You can bring the suggestion of white hairs into darker hair with short sharp marks with an eraser, but it is unlikely to make you popular with the sitter!

In older age, gravity and a lifetime of facial movements will reshape the skin and muscles of the face. The skull largely stays the same during adulthood, although it changes slightly in old age with the eye sockets becoming larger and the definition in the brow, nose, and jaw decreasing. As muscles deteriorate and gravity acts on the face over time, the skin will sag lower on the skull, often giving the face a downturned aspect. A smile will lift the face amazingly and can temporarily reverse some of the effects of gravity, making an old face seem younger.

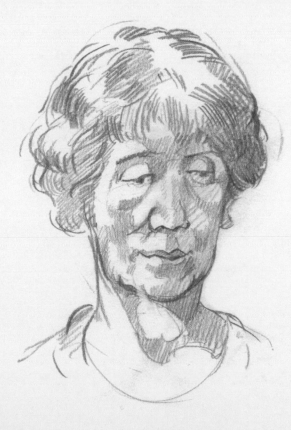

Male and Female Characteristics

Male and female faces have certain characteristics that make them appear male or female; however, all faces will contain characteristics associated with both genders and are so different that the masculine and feminine labels are often redundant. A male face may contain many female characteristics and vice versa. It is useful to understand these characteristics, as accentuating certain features can make a face appear more or less masculine or feminine, and these ideas can be used to check and alter your drawings. It is wise not to confuse typically male and female characteristics with subjective ideas of attractiveness.

a) A masculine forehead slopes back more where the feminine profile is flatter. A masculine forehead has more exaggerated ridges in the brow.
b) Feminine eyes often appear larger, due to the lighter brow ridge and more space between eyebrow and eyelid.
c) Masculine noses are often larger and longer with a large gap between the bottom of the nose and top of the lip.
d) Feminine lips are often tonally darker than the skin around them, accentuating their full shape. Masculine lips may have a similar full shape but will be tonally lighter, and so will be less prominent.
e) A masculine jaw is heavier and squarer, whereas a feminine jaw curves from earlobe to chin.
f) A man may have a prominent Adam's apple, whereas a woman's will be less prominent.
g) A feminine neck is longer, where a masculine neck is thicker and more muscular.

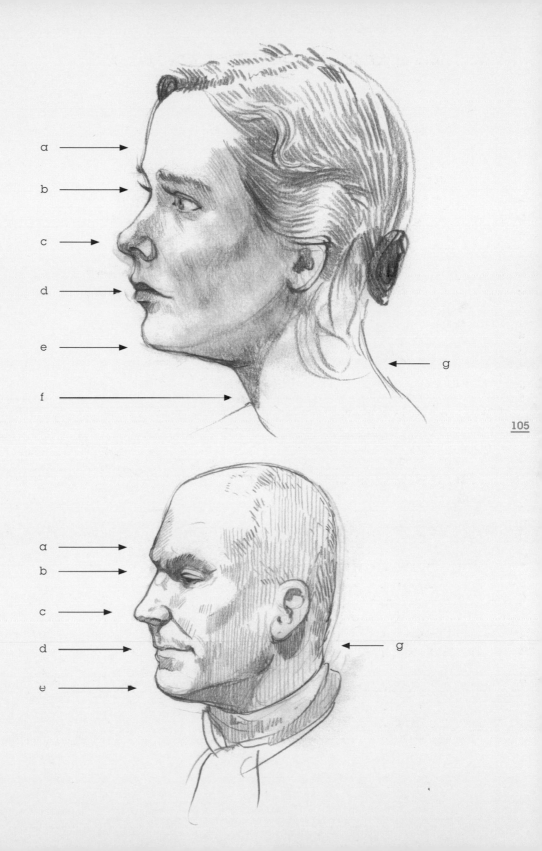

Male skull

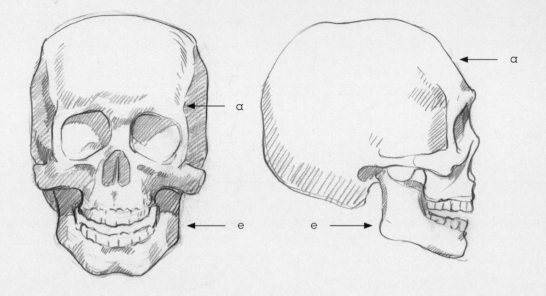

Female skull

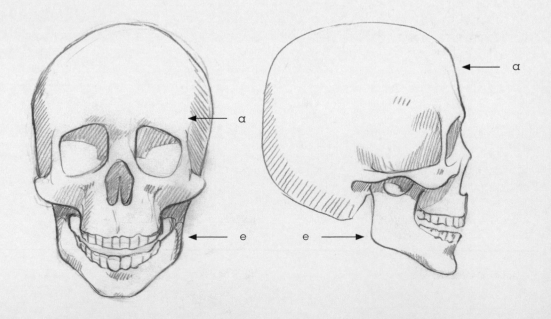

Blemishes and Freckles

Blemishes suggest something negative, but it is these notes to our uniqueness that best tell the story of who we are. When you notice scars, pock marks, and the like, there is a tendency to try to draw them in, yet sometimes they can look artificial, as if they sit on the surface of the skin. The key is to treat them much like the rest of the skin's surface: if they seem large or dark enough to warrant a mark, then put in the mark that best communicates what you see. Try not to think "there is a scar" and then draw the scar you think you see; simply make marks that replicate what you've observed.

Freckles
You can jot freckles in lightly and more sparsely than they appear on close inspection, giving a suggestion of freckles rather than overlaboring them. Again, be selective and only draw what seems significant.

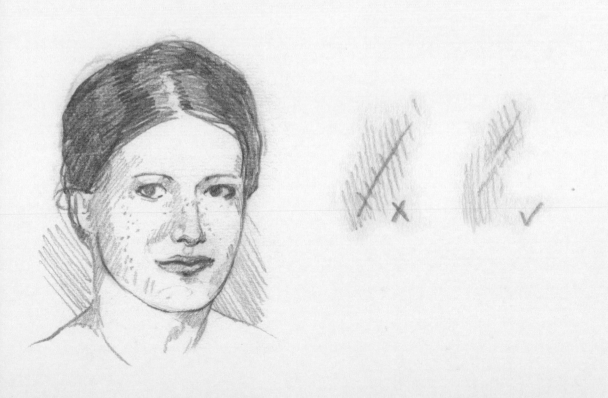

Racial Differences

Drawing is an incredible way to study a fellow human being; rarely do we ever look so closely at other people than when we are sketching them. When you've drawn a lot of people, you'll start to get a much better understanding of how the arrangement of features tells the story of your sitter's past. Their face can even betray the history of their ancestors. In a face you will see replicated the features of family members long past. People of all different races will share characteristics common to their lineage, and their faces will show the mixture of backgrounds that led to their birth.

Skin Tone

Skin tone can be important in a drawing, but it isn't so prominent as you might think. We often perceive race through facial characteristics that describe someone's racial background as much as through their skin color. A white model with a heavy tan may have tonally darker skin than a light-skinned black model. Tone is often used to communicate form and shadow much more than color; a white face in shadow will often be drawn darker than a black face in highlight. Put in the level of tone that you think will best bring out the appearance of your sitter.

Race and Proportion

Race is often much more clearly represented through the shapes and proportions of the features than the tone of the skin. The good portraitist should be far too stringent an observer to be waylaid by skin color alone, but will instead wish to understand the incredible variety that exists in all faces hung on the common themes that unite our proportions. The stereotypical variations that we use to categorize people of different races (broad, Aboriginal noses, full African lips, narrower Oriental eyes, etc.) are just a starting point for the huge variations in our facial characteristics and dimensions.

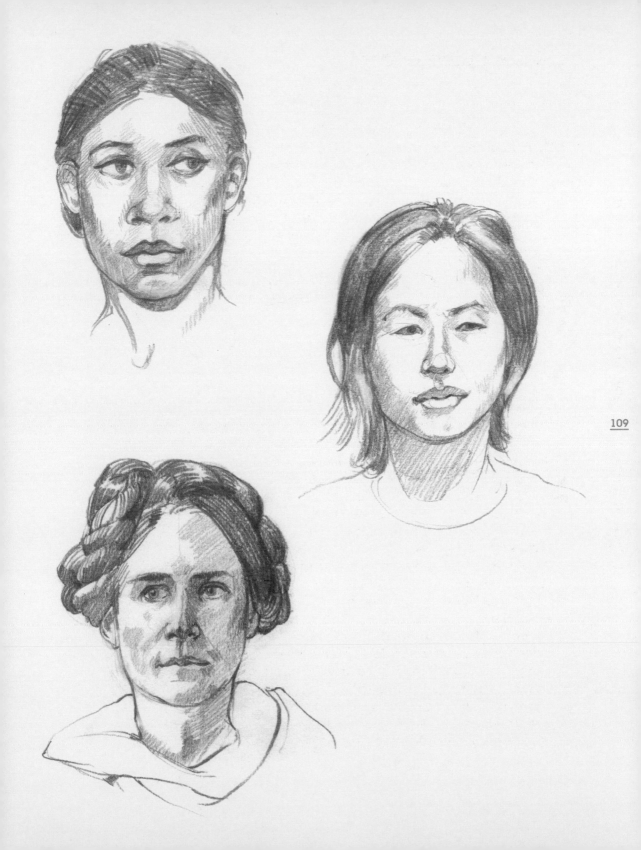

Accessories

Faces aren't always unadorned—many people have glasses, jewelry, hats, scarves, and clothes that may feature in a portrait. Here are some very simple pointers on how to deal with them

Piercings

Piercings can be simple to draw as they are often made up of very clear highlights and shadows. Leave space for the light, or bring it back in with a sharp eraser. Use clear, strong lines for the darks.

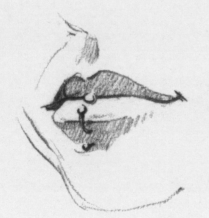

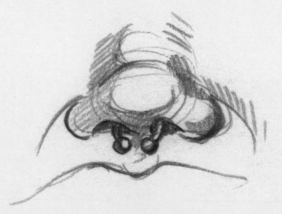

Glasses

Don't think about the shape of the glasses and try to draw them onto the head, but see how the glasses look as a part of the face. Draw them in like any other feature. This will mean going through the same stages of construction that you've gone through in previous drawings. Draw the lenses by understanding how they make the face look; if you can see a distortion in the features created by the lenses, then just draw what you see, and pay attention to any shadows that the glasses cast on the face.

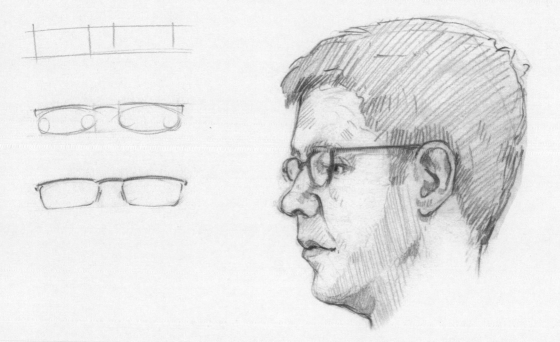

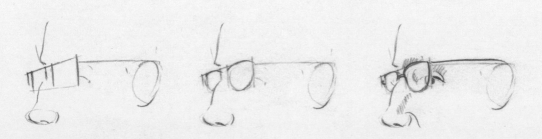

Hats

When drawing hats, look at how they interrupt the line of the forehead and bear in mind that the edge of the hat goes all the way around the head.

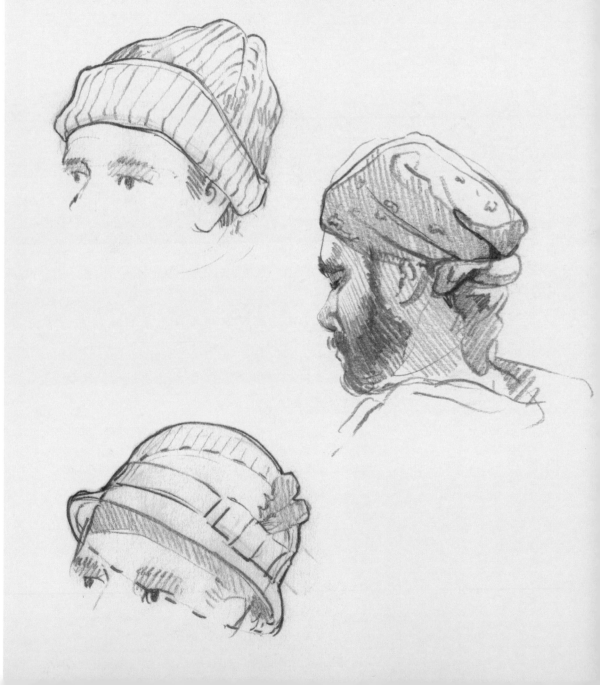

Clothes

There is another whole book to be written on drawing clothes, but for the moment just look for the big shapes that you see in the folds of cloth. Look at the shape created where the skin makes contact with the clothes, and look at the wedges of shadow between folds. Keep marks loose and patterns simple so as not to distract from the face.

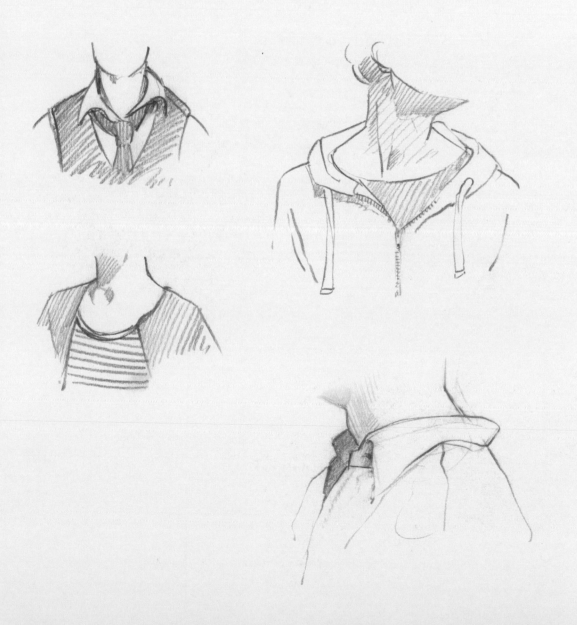

Problem Solving

The key to improving your draftsmanship is to develop the ability to look at your drawings clearly and objectively and make judgments about changes—either changes in the drawing itself or changes in your approach to future drawings. This relates to developing an internal tutor, as covered on page 18.

Looking at Your Drawing Afresh

While you're working on a drawing, it's easy to become too close to it—so close that you have trouble seeing it clearly. Develop your own strategies for looking at your drawing afresh. Step back from it, or hold it out at arm's length to compare it to the model; treat it like a "spot the difference" game, and where you identify things that might be wrong, make changes to correct them. Turning a drawing upside-down or looking at it in a mirror can be a good way of viewing the picture objectively and checking what might be wrong with it.

Dealing with a Problem

Once you've identified a problem, don't be afraid to revise your drawing. Always be prepared to erase big chunks of the drawing and redraw them—if you've drawn something once it is much easier to erase it and redraw it slightly to the left, or right, or up or down. Don't be too precious; if you really like one eye, but it is out of proportion with the rest of the face, don't try to make the drawing work around it. Erase it and make everything work together. If you don't, you'll only be unhappy with the final result anyway.

Keep your bad drawings as well as your good ones. After looking back over many drawings, you may notice that you repeat the same mistakes. This is a good thing as you can identify those mistakes and then work out how to deal with them.

Common Problems

Below and overleaf are a range of common problems, a few visual tips on how to deal with them, and page numbers in this book that might help you.

Face too big on the head (see Further Construction, p. 44; Checking Relationships, p. 54):

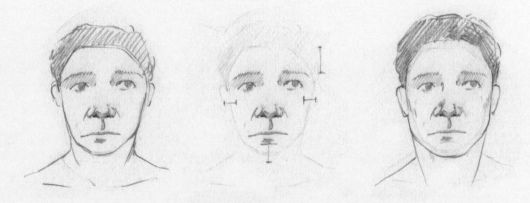

Head looks too narrow (see Understanding the Head, p. 40; Checking Relationships, p. 54):

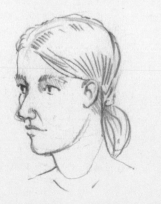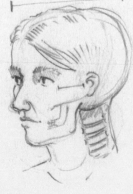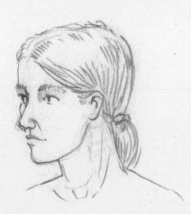

Eyes too close together (see Checking Relationships, p. 54; The Eyes, p. 72):

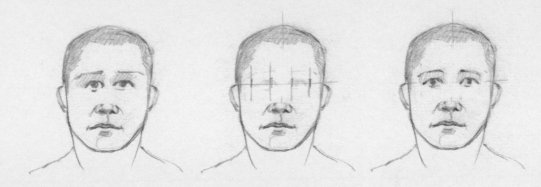

Nose looks too long (see Checking Relationships, p. 54; The Nose, p. 76):

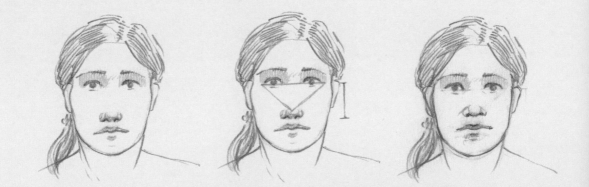

Jaw juts out too far (see Checking Relationships, p. 54; The Chin and Jaw, p. 84):

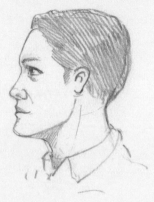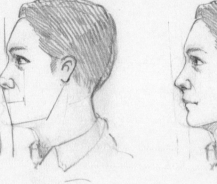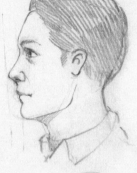

Head out of proportion with body (see Understanding the Head and Shoulders, p. 62; Negative Spaces, p. 68):

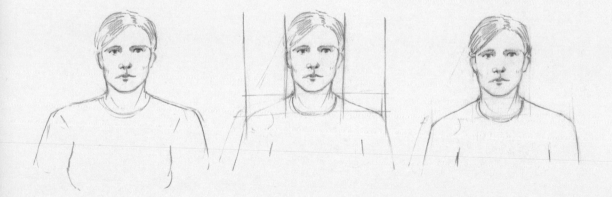

Hair Styles Reference

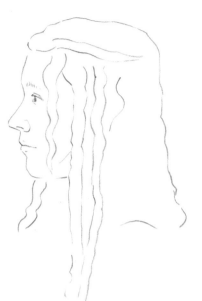

When drawing ringlets, look for the overall tube-like shape of each large ringlet, rather than drawing "curly" marks.

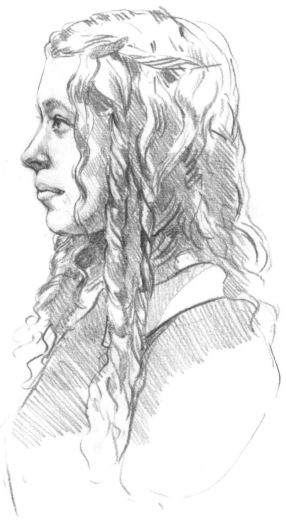

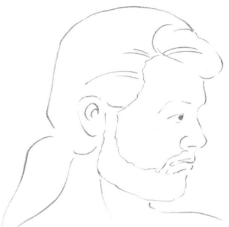

Even where textures of hair change between the face and head, start with a general outline, taking all of the areas covered by hair into account.

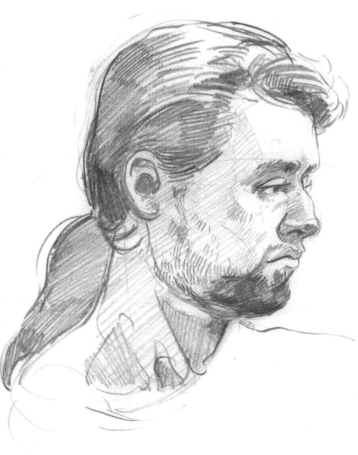

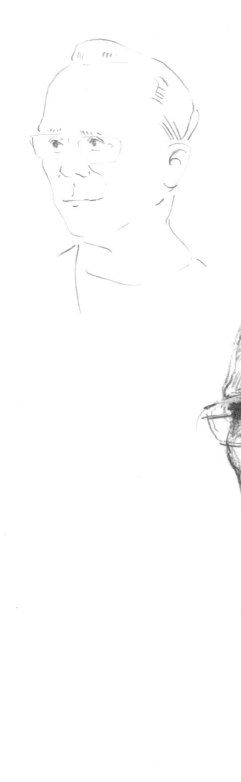

When drawing a thin, or indistinct, hairline, keep the outline light and feathered. Pay attention to how far up the forehead the hairline begins.

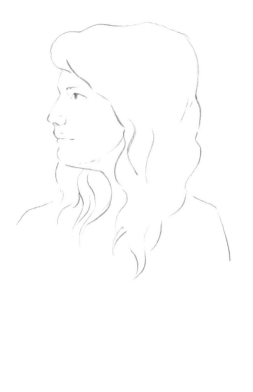

When the hair begins with distinct flows but breaks up towards the tips, block in the initial outline with general shapes and elaborate with feathered marks towards the tips of the hair.

Head Angles Reference

As the face turns away out of profile, all of the features condense into one line down the side of the face and the back of the skull becomes more prominent.

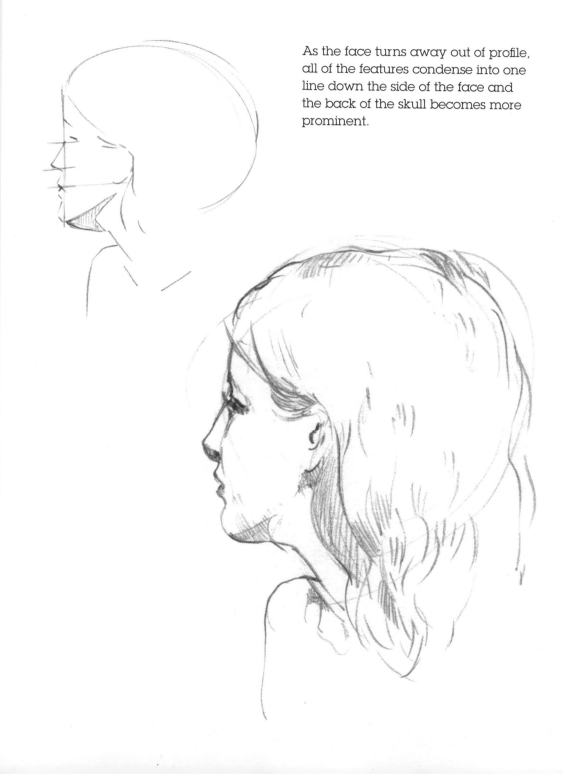

Even a slight lifting of the chin will expose the complex shadows in the neck. Use the triangle of shadow under the chin to strengthen the jawline.

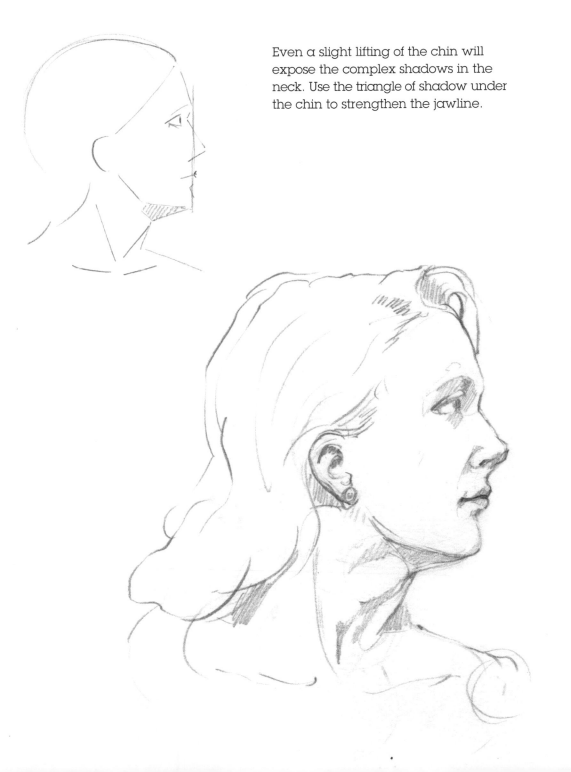

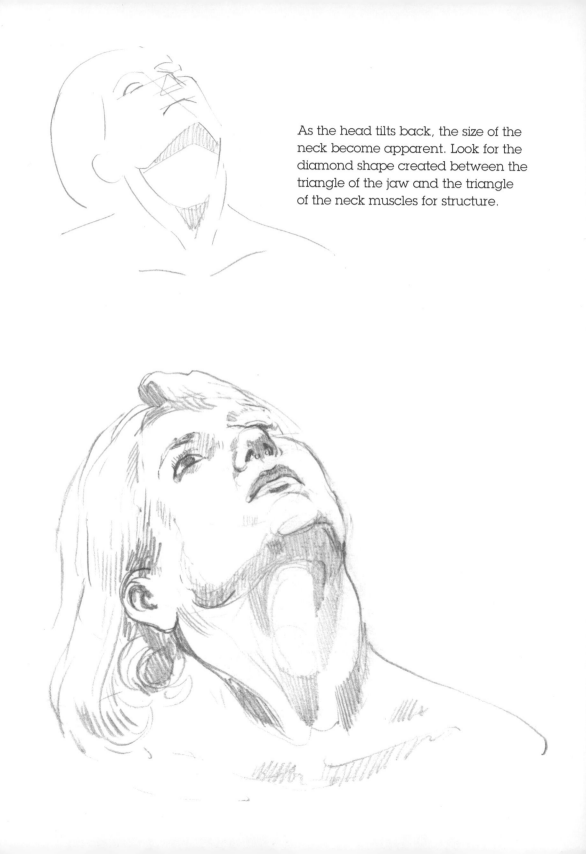

As the head tilts back, the size of the neck become apparent. Look for the diamond shape created between the triangle of the jaw and the triangle of the neck muscles for structure.

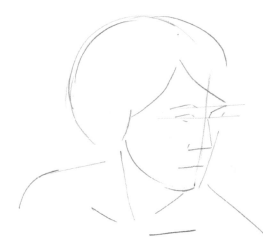

A downward tilt to the head exposes the hair on the crown on top of the head and obscures most of the shape of the neck, bringing the jaw down below the shoulders.

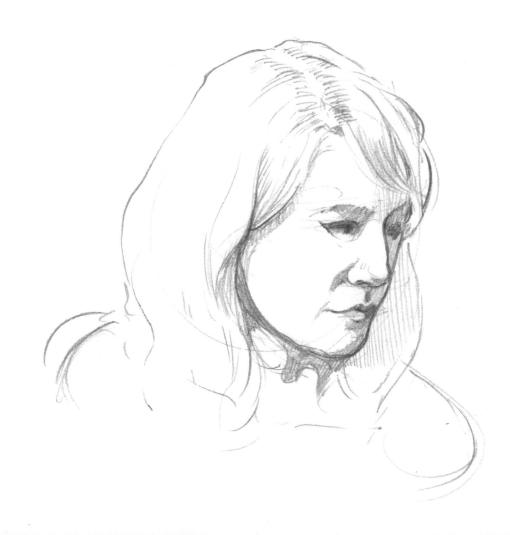

References: Exploring Drawing

If drawing portraits has given you a wider taste for drawing, here are a few tips on how to support your own drawing practice.

To progress your drawing at home, use books on drawing to support your sketching. Most importantly, spend as much time as you can looking and drawing; like any other skill, regular practice is key to maintaining your abilities. An hour a week will sustain your skills; you'll need to put in more time to make larger improvements.

By far the best way to keep improving your drawing is to find a community of other people who also love to draw. There's nothing better than finding a bunch of people who share the joyful revelations of looking and sketching and who have experienced and overcome the same obstacles inherent in learning to draw.

Many adult education centers offer structured courses in portrait or life drawing, and most towns will have small art societies. Drop-in life drawing classes and drawing clubs can be a sociable way to draw and meet others who draw, and an Internet search will often yield a wealth of groups in your area.

The international SketchCrawl movement hold regular group sketching events around the world. If you can't find anywhere suitable, consider setting up your own group, where you can take it in turns to model for portraits or share the cost of a professional artist's model. "The Draw Charter" is a pamphlet available from Draw Brighton that provides practical advice on setting up your own drawing class. To share your drawings on Facebook, Twitter or Instagram with the author and other enthusiasts add the hashtag #drawfaces.

You can't beat the opportunities to share tips and techniques that a drawing class can provide.

Practical Drawing Books

Portrait Drawing
by John T. Freeman

The Natural Way to Draw
by Kimon Nicolaides

Keys to Drawing
by Bert Dodson

Drawing on the Right Side of the Brain
by Betty Edwards

The Draw Charter
by Jake Spicer

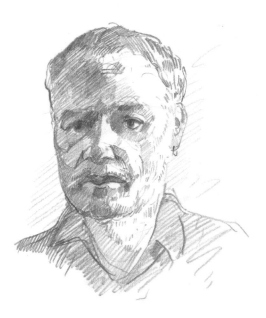

Online Resources

SketchCrawl
www.sketchcrawl.com

Draw Brighton
www.draw-brighton.co.uk

Jake Spicer
www.jakespicerart.co.uk

Social Media

@BrightonDrawing
#drawfaces

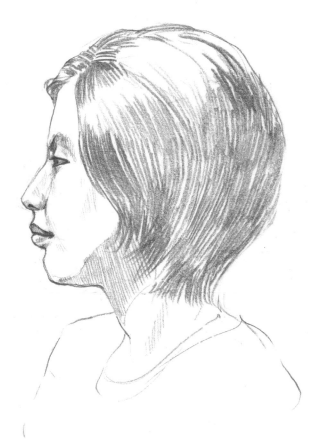

Acknowledgments

This book owes particular thanks to Duncan Cromarty, who gave his time, advice, and experience with customary generosity.

I'd also like to thank John T. Freeman and Jane Alison for starting it all, Tammy Cherriman and my family for their support, and Shelley Morrow and Laura Burgess for keeping the studio running. Special thanks should also go to Lucy Clougherty, Jenni Creswell, and Mary Martin for their help, and to Emma Sandham King, Francesca Cluney, Naomi Mcleod, Amy Squirrel, Ian Lowe, Keith Mercer, Felix Clement Parker, Ottavio Pedretti, Naomi Wood, Alison Milner Gulland, Peggy Squire, Vicky Bloodworth, Chris Keeley, Rosie Kirk, Alice Richardson, Colette Tarbuck, Jene, Chiara, Issy, and Juno for having such wonderful faces. Finally, thank you to Ellie, Zara, and especially Nick at Ilex for sticking with me.